P9-AOY-656

DATE DUE

GREEN POWER:

THE
CORPORATION
AND THE
URBAN CRISIS

GREEN POWER:
THE CORPORATION AND THE URBAN CRISIS

George S. Odiorne

Pitman Publishing Corporation

New York   Toronto   London   Tel Aviv

Contents

HD
59
034
c. 2

T43 F 71

SX

1   *America Will Burn*   **3**

2   *Will the Urban Crisis Go Away?*   **19**

3   *Can Government Solve the Problem?*   **32**

4   *Is Riot Control the Answer?*   **48**

5   *The Military Services as a Possible Solution*   **62**

6   *Can Some New Way Be Developed?*   **78**

7   *Is Black Power a Solution?*   **89**

8   *The Negro Market—A Positive Reason
    for Business Action*   **99**

9   *Action at the Top*   **113**

10 *Middle Management Programs*   **130**

11 *Responsibilities of the Foreman*   **142**

12 *The Rocky Road Ahead*   **157**

Appendix: Memorandum from Henry Ford II
            to Ford Motor Company Management   **179**

Notes to Chapters   **183**

Bibliography   **186**

Index   **189**

Preface

This is not a book for social workers; it's a book for businessmen and students of business. It is a hard-nosed book. It might also be called a book for conservatives—the kind of people who would preserve the system because they own it or run it and are its beneficiaries. If you are a hard-nosed businessman you aren't on any kind of crusade. You do want to see the system survive, work well, and prosper. To do that you will hire the hard-core unemployable, ex-convicts, drop-outs, those who have already flunked your tests and interviews.

This book looks at all the alternatives, and from a business viewpoint finds no other. You *must* hire them. This doesn't mean you merely write a neat policy: "We will hire any qualified applicant who comes in"; that's outmoded. Your employment manager may be adhering to a nice array of little procedures that aren't worth the paper they are written on. The process now is *select them in*, not out.

As you read, be as critical as you like. If you want to be successful in business, you'll hire "the unemployable," even if you have to trek up the tenement stairs and get them. If you want to get a practical corporation viewpoint, read on.

Ann Arbor, Michigan   George S. Odiorne
February 1969

GREEN POWER:

THE CORPORATION AND THE URBAN CRISIS

1

AMERICA WILL BURN

We do not have the power to overthrow,
but the riots prove that we have the
power to disrupt—to burn.
Daniel H. Watts,
THE SATURDAY EVENING POST

Shortly after the assassination of Martin Luther King, Jr., federal employees from offices in Washington were on their way home to the suburbs. The streets and bridges to places like Arlington, Bethesda, and Silver Spring were jammed with cars filled with frightened people. As Congressman James Harvey of Michigan described it:

We were heading for Bethesda, several congressmen of the United States in one sedan. All around us we could see our nation's capital in flames. As traffic ground to a halt, gangs of Negro youths swarmed around the stalled vehicles, pounding on the hoods and fenders with their fists. "Run, honky, run, we going to kill ya," they shouted. I was never more frightened in my life.[1]

Few people who have lived through the riots of 1967 and 1968 have forgotten them. The chairman of General Motors

3

on July 23, 1967, looked out of his windows over the city of Detroit and saw it burning in a ring around the horizon.[2] The city was "saturated with fear,"[3] reported two generals in charge of troops dispatched to quell the riot. A spirit of genial and reckless anarchy seemed to take hold of the rioters. Young men were reported to be "dancing among the flames."

A leader of the black community took up a bull horn to talk to his people, and had a rock hurled at his head. The firemen who came to extinguish the blaze were fired upon, and finally ordered to withdraw if fired upon again. The chronology shows a rising level of violent protest in the black community:[4]

1963: Riots involving whites and blacks occurred in Birmingham, Savannah, Cambridge, Md., Chicago, and Philadelphia. Mobs battled each other and the police. White retaliation took the form of bombing, including that of a black church where four young black girls were killed while attending Sunday School.

1964: White response to black activity resulted in riots and violence in Jacksonville, and the Molotov cocktail was used for the first time. In Cleveland a bulldozer ran over and killed a young white minister picketing for civil rights. More violence followed. In Mississippi, three white civil rights workers were lynched, and in Harlem blacks battled police for several days; riots spread to Brooklyn. In Rochester, N.Y., two days of violence required that the National Guard be called in. Philadelphia underwent two nights of rioting following the arrest of a black woman for insulting two policemen.

4

1965: A mixture of black and white civil rights workers marched in Selma, Ala., a paper city, and were dispersed by the police. A white clergyman and Detroit housewife active in civil rights were slain. In Bogalusa, La., another paper town, whites attacked blacks. The most serious of the riots to date and a model for others to follow occurred in the Watts section of Los Angeles. A confrontation between police and blacks led to three days of burning and looting, which were finally arrested by the National Guard. Thirty-four persons were killed, hundreds more were injured, and nearly 4,000 persons were arrested. Snipers were reported active, and damage to property was estimated at $35 million. As the nation's worst riot since the Detroit riots of 1943 in which 43 died on Belle Isle, Watts shocked the nation.

1966: New riots erupted in Watts in May of the following year, the participants mainly young people. In July of that year a minor incident between police and black youths in Chicago erupted into a riot, with firebombing, looting, and rock-throwing going on until put down by 4,200 National Guardsmen. Three died and hundreds were injured.

A week later in the Hough section of Cleveland, a riot erupted in which four were killed; sniping was reported, with reports of instigators fanning the flames of discord.

Forty-three major and minor disorders of the black communities of the nation were reported that year.

1967: The rioting started this year in the spring at three Southern universities for blacks: Fisk University, Tennessee Agricultural and Industrial College, and Jackson State in Mississippi. Rock-throwing, Molotov cocktails, and confrontations with police were in evidence at all three. In Houston black picket lines being controlled by police erupted into violence. In Tampa a youth was shot by a policeman, and a full-scale riot was averted by action of public officials and a white-hatted Youth Patrol of black young men. In June, after several confrontations of police and blacks, Cincinnati erupted, with burnings, dozens injured and hundreds arrested before the riot was put down by the Ohio National Guard. In Atlanta in June two were killed and others injured following a confrontation between blacks and police.

In July the major riot of the year up to that time broke out in Newark, N.J. The arrest of a cab driver produced a mob of blacks around a police station, where Molotov cocktails were thrown. For several nights thereafter the Central Ward became a battleground, with reports of snipers, heavy damage to businesses and homes due to fire, and 23 deaths —two whites and 21 blacks. Property damage came to an estimated $10 million. The disorders spread to the neighboring cities of Jersey City, Elizabeth, New Brunswick, and Plainfield. The nation was aghast at the ferocity of the rioting, the damage, the killing, and the burning. But the worst still lay ahead.

In Detroit a routine raid on a "blind pig" (an unlicensed drinking club) on Twelfth Street early Sunday morning produced reaction from the black inhabitants of the area. The disturbance accelerated rapidly and raced across many square miles of Detroit. Forty-three people died before the Michigan National Guard, bolstered by a regiment of federal paratroopers, restored order. Fire companies were

6

fired upon as they fought the fires. More than 7,000 persons were arrested, looting was rampant, and insurance losses on property damage were finally estimated at $32 million.

For the year, the subcommittee on investigations of the Senate Committee on Government Operations concluded that there were 75 disturbances in 67 cities, causing 83 deaths and 1,897 injuries. The damage to property through burning and looting ran over $90 million. The high costs to public and governmental agencies should be added to this. Beyond this were the inestimable damage to public confidence and the growth of fear, suspicion, and hostility.

1968: Violence erupted once again, earlier than in prior years, following the assassination of Dr. Martin Luther King, Jr. The capital of the United States became the focal point of the worst of the early riots, but the violence was not only there. The rifleman who shot King set off looting and fire-bombing over the whole nation. Block after block of slums in Washington, Pittsburgh, Chicago, and Baltimore were burned out. Incidents of varying intensity occurred in Oakland, Nashville, Tallahassee, Richmond, Topeka, Buffalo, Battle Creek, and dozens of other cities. Retail stores were hit especially hard, even stores in the uptown locations which had been spared the year before. Only a few blocks from the White House, rioters rolled down F Street selectively looting jewelry, men's wear, and radio-television shops. In the Seventh Street area, where merchants had acquired a reputation for overpriced goods and high interest rates, the looting was more extensive. The National Retail Merchants Association issued an emergency bulletin to members.

Security forces provide no effective safeguard to the retailers in the cases of serious and widespread acts of violence. The police are frequently outnumbered and when the military is called in it is frequently too late.

In New York numerous small chains around the city were robbed of shoes, clothes, and appliances. Stores in East St. Louis and in Pittsburgh's Hill section were heavily hit. In Baltimore "looters hit everything in sight," according to one report. In Chicago a two-mile stretch on the West Side was leveled.

The American Insurance Association, an organization of property insurance companies, put the damage figure at about $30 million, which, for a four-day stretch, started 1968 off with damage equal in value to that of almost half of the entire year 1967.

Over 21,000 troops from federal forces and 45,000 National Guardsmen were employed, with many more in reserve. In Washington, D.C., alone 12,000 troops were in the city and 4,000 more in reserve. Machine guns were mounted on the steps of the Capitol building. The death rate per riot was down considerably, with only ten deaths in Washington, for example; probably the decrease was a direct product of the policy of "Let 'em loot and don't shoot." Six thousand persons were arrested in Washington, and 1,000 reported injured, mostly blacks. In those cities, such as Kansas City and Trenton, where a looter was shot, the action was followed by increased crowd activity, retaliatory assaults, and burnings.

By the first week in July the pattern of police reaction

was apparent. In Washington, D.C., firm action against the "poor people" demonstrators was followed by a riot among Washington blacks, which was quickly and forcefully crushed. The residents of Resurrection City were ordered to pick up and leave after their permit expired on June 23. Defiance by the leaders led to mass arrests. Up at 14th and U streets where the massive riots of spring had occurred, 2,000 people were in the streets, apparently ready to pick up where they had left off. Bricks flew at police and passing cars, store windows shattered. The riot control forces moved in 1,500 police backed by 1,500 National Guardsmen, with another 1,500 federals in reserve. Tear gas grenades flew into the streets by the hundreds, and the streets themselves were swept free of mobs. Three hundred were arrested, and one looter was shot. Black Mayor Walter Washington clapped on a 9 P.M. curfew, and violators were arrested. By midnight the city was silent and calm.

Congressmen hailed the success of the new methods. The president of the United States Chamber of Commerce, Winton M. Blount, hailed the success of the new display of force. "We saw it work," he stated.[5] Through early July a rash of minor incidents broke out. They were quickly publicized by a press which seemed hungry for news of disorderly blacks. One hundred young blacks in Minneapolis threw firebombs, and a handful were arrested; five were injured over the Fourth of July holiday. Young blacks threw rocks and bottles in Memphis, and a Catholic store in the Homewood section of Pittsburgh was firebombed. Paterson, N.J. was the scene of the first summer struggles. In a predominantly Puerto Rican section, a man was arrested for splashing water from an open hydrant on passing motorists. The incident led to a fight after which a policeman received 42 stitches. Five nights of disorder followed. With 18,000 Puerto Ricans and 30,000 blacks, Paterson was the first city outside Harlem where racial groups other than blacks rioted.

The reaction of Paterson police proved, in a reverse kind of way, the efficacy of the newly developed tactics. There was no fast response, no curfew, no clearing of the streets after dark. The use of Spanish-speaking priests and others to lessen tensions through talking seemed to be the major effort. Fifty were arrested.

Even before all the results were tallied, studies by the United States Department of Justice and by the Lemberg Center for the Study of Violence at Brandeis University revealed that 1968 was a more violent year than 1967, the previous year with the most disturbances. While new police methods of managing riots have apparently succeeded in reducing the number of mass disorders, the Lemberg Center reported, the new methods have not reduced the number of disorders, which by August 1968 were double that of the entire year before.

While rioting and deaths attributable to it went down in 1968, the new pattern of smaller disturbances was costlier in terms of property damage than in any previous year. The American Insurance Association reported that property damage for insured losses in the first eight months of 1968 exceeded the total losses for insured property due to civil disturbances in all of 1967.

The rise in property damage and the decline in deaths

10

have been accompanied by an increase in the number of incidents involving shooting at the police. In 1968 gunfire attacks upon police in such cities as Cleveland, Cincinnati, Gary, New York City, Peoria, and Seattle, over fifty policemen were killed or wounded.

The Basic Process of a Riot

One pattern which has been common to most disturbances is described by the Kerner Commission.[6]

a. *An accumulation of grievances* in the black community which are often unknown to the people in power. These generally include poor job opportunities, bad housing, inability to move from such housing even when employed, frustrated aspirations of many members of the black community, and a sense of rage over inability to effect changes. This generates the steam for the explosion of violence to follow.

b. *A triggering incident,* usually involving police and a black who is done a real or fancied injustice by the law. Most such incidents are trivial in themselves, but coupled with an underlying frustration and discontent they rapidly become the starting point of disorders. Usually the specific incident is the latest in a series of prior incidents which have grated on the sensibilities of the population.

These add up to the next stage.

c. *Violence and disorder.* While there is no uniform pat-

11

tern to the violence which ensues, there are some general trends.

1. Violence normally occurs in locations where conditions are congested, people are in the streets, and traffic flow is dense. It tends to occur in the evening when people are not at work, often on weekends.

2. It is more apt to occur when the temperature is high, and the undesirable conditions of the slum are more apparent, with its foul odors, uncomfortable living quarters, and crowded streets.

3. Violence mounts as word spreads, more youngsters gravitate to the scene, and minor crowds turn first to looting, then to property damage, and finally to personal injury.

d. *Control efforts.* The pattern of control efforts usually begins with attempts by the police to clear the area, using force or threats of force. Where rioting continues or grows, supplemental military forces are called or their call is threatened. These activities are supplemented by negotiations with civil rights leaders, often with the use of conciliation and persuasion by counterrioters on the street.

According to the Kerner Commission Report, the rioter himself is not often the lowest economic category of black. Most often he is a high school drop-out, between 15 and 25 years old, with a job, but working below the skill level which he feels is appropriate to his qualifications.

The majority of the 1967 rioters were single, about 25 percent were illegitimate, and three out of four were born in the North. Income generally ran below $5,000 per year. Ninety percent of the rioters had finished grade school, although few had finished high school. A high percentage of rioters had experienced unemployment during the prior year, and their employment was apt to be in unskilled service or the less desirable, low-paying factory positions. They attributed these low-status jobs to racial discrimination. Three-quarters of the rioters reported that they hate white people, and almost as many hate middle-class blacks. Rioters tended to be more active in the civil rights area than nonrioters from the same area.[7]

What Do the Facts Mean to the Manager?

We have seen the bare facts. What do they imply for the manager in a modern business? What do they imply for him as a citizen, and as a businessman? While it would be foolish to try to separate the two—citizenship and managerial responsibility—this book looks at the problem from a purely business and managerial viewpoint. In part this is because if the two are inextricable the conclusions should be similar. In part this approach is invaluable because so many managers fail to see the problem as one which must be solved mainly by the corporation and its managers if it is to be solved at all.

The thesis of this book is simply put. The problem and its solution rest with business and its managers, and the solution is inescapably a management responsibility.

13

Here the value of taking a purely hardheaded business approach pays off. The reason for businessmen to move hard and fast to solve the urban crisis is not a "do-good" motive. This is not a favor the business community is doing for the government, or the hard-core ghetto dweller.

It is a favor the businessman does himself, given the business objective of profit and growth. Even if you are an opponent of the idea that business has a social responsibility, you should see that solving the urban crisis is one of the greatest business opportunities of our time, with a tangible payoff for business when it is accomplished.

In the ensuing chapters we shall examine the alternative ways of solving the problem, and conclude that no existing method stands a chance of solving it, except a massive business effort led by hard-nosed managers.

What are the alternative business reactions to the urban crisis?

A number of possible alternatives for the business firm and its management present themselves. They include these:

Alternative 1. *Do nothing.* Often problems go away if left alone and ignored for a decent interval. Population figures, together with rising pride in race and rising levels of aspiration, indicate that this one won't.

Alternative 2. *Let things burn.* The evidence of four years of disorder indicates that disorder feeds on itself. The property destruction alone makes it impossible to ignore from a business viewpoint. Business goes to pot when people are

14

looting. In the week following the assassination of Martin Luther King, Jr., auto sales fell 20 percent. Lost production, rising costs to government agencies to quell disorders, interrupted business—all make the disorders something which from a purely business viewpoint can't be ignored. Even if you choose to overlook the social and human consequences of riots, you are obviously faced with a business problem of some dimensions; and when a business manager is faced with a problem he cannot simply forget it; something must be done.

Alternative 3. *Let the government do it.* Some managers may pass the buck back to the federal or state government, or perhaps the local police force or human relations commission. The major hitch in this solution is in the high taxation that would be required to support the massive program that would be necessary. Manpower programs, economic opportunity programs, and the like have an exorbitant cost per person, and the amount needed would soon run beyond our tax tolerance. Representative Wilbur Mills of Arkansas, chairman of the House Ways and Means Committee, became the hero of our time in the spring of 1968 with his defense against a tax rise. As a businessman and a manager you simply can't afford to let the problem be handled through government, for which you must pay the bill.

Alternative 4. *Put down disorders with riot control forces, including police marshals, National Guard, and if necessary federal troops.* The upper limit here is set by the amount of force we are willing to let police and troops use on citizens, and by the self-feeding nature of force. Ultimately such a basic answer if relied upon exclusively calls for gas chambers, or, as one congressional committee proposed, internment camps. A major problem here is that authorizing such total use of force puts power in the hands of people who might not limit themselves to rioters. They might start using their power on others, for example, Republicans. Clearly this is an unthinkable solution.

Alternative 5. *New and innovative programs might be developed which would do the job.* Many examples come to mind. The citizens of city X found that they had some discontented unemployed who were getting themselves in trouble, so they worked up a little demonstration project which found jobs for about fifty such persons and thus shunted them off from making trouble. Many cities have tried these small demonstration projects. While they are all laudable and undoubtedly do much good within the local situation, as a systematic way of attacking a gross social ill they are inadequate. They are too small and lack depth, scope, and the power to sustain their effort. Once their initial burst of enthusiasm and publicity is past, people notice that they cost too much, and they tend to fade away.

Alternative 6. *Business could hire the rioters and train them.* The experience of World War II, in which 13 million previously unemployed persons were inducted and trained to do work in war factories, with spectacular results, demonstrates that industry and business have the capacity to hire and train them. Not only will this alternative be faster and cheaper than any other, but it will eliminate many undesirable side effects of the other alternatives. There are subproblems in following Alternative 6 which managers must work out for themselves, but they are soluble and have in fact been solved in Detroit since the summer disorders of 1967.

The high costs of the other alternatives can best be highlighted by matching them against Alternative 6. One solution is to put them all in the army. The former Secretary of Defense seems to have been in partial agreement with this solution, since the military has a policy of inducting unqualified men and giving them special literacy and other physical mental upgrading. Yet who in management ranks will profess enthusiasm for a five-million-man black army made up of young men who fit the profile of the rioter?

Beyond the six alternatives listed above are others, far too unreal and farfetched to merit separate consideration here as serious business proposals. Ship them all back to Africa, shoot the bastards, let 'em starve, and similar emotional spasms of the unthinking are not serious proposals, but visceral reactions. As serious business managers, we choose from one of the six, or some combination of them. What makes the sixth alternative, "Hire them," the only responsible solution?

1. The major reason is that the others have been tried in whole or in part and simply haven't worked at all.

2. There are massive opportunities for business if it solves the problems: higher profits, greater growth, and a stable society in which orderly legitimate business can prosper.

Note that this isn't a social or ethical appeal, but a business approach. Let's look at it from that viewpoint. We'll skip for now the obvious facts that we are in the 178th year of the Bill of Rights and the 21st year of the Declara-

17

tion of Human Rights of the United Nations, that we are a nation with a traditional respect for the individual, and so on. The appeal here is a managerial one. If you still need some convincing, let's look at the alternatives in a little more detail and see the paucity of evidence in favor of the first five and the managerial good sense in the sixth—*hiring them.*

After that we'll deal with what you do to implement Alternative 6, and what the experience of others has been who have tried it in the world's largest corporations and made it work.

18

2

WILL THE URBAN CRISIS GO AWAY?

All I want is for you to vanish into the
ground! I need peace. I'd give up the
world for a kopek just to be left in peace.
           Fyodor Dostoyevsky,
    NOTES FROM UNDERGROUND

Commenting on the current rash of student uprisings, a college president reportedly stated that "there is no student problem that can't be solved in four years." There is some evidence that the urban crisis and disorders won't follow such a pattern. The poverty of the blacks is the result of a long buildup, and is deeply rooted in some trends that promise to worsen before they get better. Essentially it is perpetuated by six factors which could lead to social (and business) disaster.

   1. The urbanization of blacks, and at the same time the flight of whites from the city.

   2. The different rates of population growth between blacks and whites, with the former increasing faster than the latter.

   3. Higher levels of unemployment among blacks.

   4. Widespread, devastating poverty among urban blacks.

   5. The decline of family life, health, and welfare among urban blacks.

19

6. An increased unwillingness to accept existing conditions and a rising ability to organize to fight them through action programs.

These comprise a sequence which is well established and cannot be reversed because the basic urbanization is already well developed and is impossible to undo. Let's examine these stages in a little more detail.

Urbanization of Blacks

Today some 15 million of a total population of 21.5 million blacks live in metropolitan areas, and at the same time there is a migration from the South northward. This northward, city-bound movement has been the pattern since 1910, with the single decade of largest migration during the war years when labor shortages attracted southern blacks to jobs in the North. The pattern of this migration is shown in Table 1.

Table 1
Pattern of Urban Migration

DESTINATION—CITIES	AREA OF ORIGIN
1. Boston, New York, Philadelphia, Baltimore, Washington, D.C.	Georgia, Florida, the Carolinas, Alabama
2. Detroit, Chicago, Cleveland, Cincinnati	Mississippi, Tennessee, Alabama, Louisiana, Arkansas
3. Los Angeles	Texas, Louisiana, Alabama, Mississippi, Arkansas

Simultaneously the urbanization of blacks has accrued in Southern cities as well. Today, our estimate from most currently available census figures of the percentage of the

20

total black population living in cities would be slightly over 70. One American city, Washington, D.C., has a black population majority. Newark, Atlanta, Memphis, and New Orleans are over 40 percent black. Detroit, Philadelphia, Baltimore, Houston, Cleveland, and St. Louis are between 30 and 40 percent black. Twenty-six percent of the population of our cities of over one million is black, as opposed to 13 percent of the total population of the United States.

During the period from 1950 to 1966, census figures reveal that the white population of cities declined rapidly: 10.7 million whites left central cities during those sixteen years. Most of this movement was due to normal turnover, the formation of new families outside the cities rather than inside, and the attraction of the suburbs with their better living conditions. Suburbs have remained predominantly white, with a black population in the fringes of cities actually declining from 5 percent to 4 percent over the period from 1960 to 1966. This in part can be attributed to bias, but even more importantly to the inability of blacks to afford the higher cost of living in suburbia, even where biased sales or rental arrangements were not significant.

The suburban commuter goes into the city each day to work, only to flee on commuter trains or by freeway back to the white bedroom communities when the day is over, leaving the inner city, with increasing frequency, to the black.

Population Growth of Blacks

The reproduction rate of black women has long been

21

greater than that of white women. For many years this difference in the rate of live births between blacks and whites was offset by the immigration of white Europeans, which actually caused the percentage of blacks in the total population to decrease. The decline of white immigration after 1920 produced a rise in the percentage of the population which was black. From 1909 to 1966 the population increase in the United States was twice as high among blacks as among whites. Thus, while the black population of the United States is now 13 percent of the total population, by 1972 it will rise to 16 percent.

The most important single factor for the future is the ages of the population and the fact that the black segment is generally younger than the white. Today about one baby in six born is black.

In the cities it is possible to estimate with some accuracy that 30 percent or more of the population under ten years old is black, and that in the nation as a whole the black population under ten years of age is about 18 percent, and will reach 20 percent by 1970.

The old Jesuit saying, "Give me a youngster until he is six years old and I don't care who has him the rest of his life," comes to mind. Just who has "had" these youngsters who make up 20 percent of our population under ten during those formative years? A look at the quality of life in the urban ghetto would indicate that it has not been parents, teachers, or youth group leaders, but the pimps, the hustlers, the dope-pushers, the gang leaders.

From time to time we'll refer again to that 20 percent of the population under ten years of age. It makes the rest of this report seem like a race to escape a problem that has a head start of a good ten years or more. Those children comprise the most persuasive evidence in answer to the question posed at the head of this chapter: "Will the urban crisis go away?" On the contrary, it will gain after a ten-year head start, and the implications of this fact for society in general and business—which is the focus of this book—are ominous.

Unemployment Among Blacks

As unemployment among the entire population has gone down, unemployment among blacks has gone down also. However, at a rate estimated at 8 percent in 1966 (with no appreciable change evident at this writing, but with a de- cline probable), the proportion of unemployed blacks is twice that of whites. For married black males the rate is 3 percent; but the jobs they hold are in a majority of cases lowest-level positions, as operatives, in unskilled or semi-skilled labor, or in service. Over a third of those blacks employed receive wages that place them in the "poverty" category.

In the cities, where three-quarters of the blacks live, the unemployment rate approaches a depression level. Job-lessness is further concentrated heavily among the younger blacks, between 16 and 19 years of age. One estimate is that one-third in this age bracket is unemployed.

An even larger number are in the category of "underemployed." This means that they take part-time and temporary jobs doing such things as passing handbills, carwashing, and casual labor. The effects here are twofold:

1. The men are not occupied and must fill their days and nights with other matters, such as standing on street corners or taking part in hustling engagements along the lines of numbers-running, dope-pushing, or seeking something for nothing. The deteriorating and explosive effects of this are of course not confined to blacks. In 1932, when unemployment rates ran in this range among whites, unrest and ugly disorders were not uncommon. The corroding effect of unemployment and underemployment is evidenced by the high number of the underemployed young who take part in riots. From TV they learn that America is prosperous. Their own sense of failure in the midst of surrounding success was summarized by one black youth interviewed by this writer who stated, "We aren't bothered by a depression, we're failures during the boom." At the same time they are feeling a rising pride in their color ("Black is beautiful") and the sense of power that has come from white attention aroused by the disorders of the past four years.

2. The lack of full employment leaves this key group short of their aspirations for the material things that are flaunted before them on TV and in movies.

Ray Marshall, professor of economics at the University of Texas, has expressed the unemployment problem this way:

Although there are important noneconomic causes of racial tension, there can be little doubt that job opportunities are

24

central concerns of Negroes and whites. The white workers' hostility toward Negroes is caused in part by fear of job competition. But the impact of inadequate jobs is much more serious for Negroes. And the problem is not only in terms of dollars, but in terms of poor health, broken families, high rates of crime, squalid housing, personal degradation, and misery.[1]

In July 1964 *The New York Times* surveyed black districts in New York City and found that economic concerns such as jobs and pay are the biggest problem that blacks have to worry about. Matters such as freedom, discrimination, racial bias, and the like were considered a major worry by only 16 percent of the respondents.

The solution for business, however, isn't going to be finding jobs for the dangerous 20 percent under ten years of age, or solely finding jobs for teen-agers. The process must be one of finding jobs for qualified but underemployed blacks to move all of them up the ladder in stair-step fashion. By underemployment of qualified blacks a compression of the entry positions is caused, and the end effect is explosive in its impact on the young.

Even the easing of biased or exclusive hiring policies which has occurred in many firms (and a few government agencies) will not solve the problem immediately. Among the underemployed there is a tendency to settle for certain low-level employment rather than for uncertain promotion. A taxi driver in Washington, D.C. with a B.A. degree from Wayne State University told the writer in an interview:

At least I am sure that this job won't fold up under me when the going gets rough. With a degree I think I can talk my way

25

into holding onto a taxi-driving job at least. If I took a job with a company or a government agency I might do better for a while, but with the first economic downturn or RIF [reduction in force in a government agency] I'd be back on the street. It happened to me once over in the ——— Agency, and it isn't going to happen again.

If indeed the problem won't go away of its own accord, today's manager in a large corporation can be assured even further that it won't be made to go away simply by stating a policy, as was explained soberly to the author by a vice president of a large firm:

> Yes indeed, I agree we have a problem, and as a result we have changed our policies so that we will be pleased—even eager—to hire any qualified applicant who applies.

The magnitude of this man's misperception of the situation is staggering. Perhaps the declaration of Henry Ford II, who clearly sees the problem, that "any businessman who doesn't see that business must move in on the problem is stupid" is strong, but nonetheless it is plausible, and even convincing.[2] Those who have seen their city burning or smelled the smoke of the ruins of Twelfth Street in Detroit or Madison Street in Chicago have learned. Their conversion has not been on the road to Damascus like St. Paul's, but on the road to ruin.

Poverty Amid Riches

A consequence of the rising population, migration to the

cities, and unemployment among these gathered gro
has been a special kind of problem: the existence of a
polarized society, separate but unequal. In many ways this
is more than a black and white polarization. Many of the
black middle class are better off than they ever were before, and some "have it made." At the same time this division between black classes causes a chasm between black
leadership and the ghetto dweller who lives in poverty.

To assume that the problem will simply dry up and go
away, that the 20 percent under ten years of age who are
learning life values in the urban ghetto will "vanish into the
ground" and leave the middle class in peace amidst their
lawns and split levels, is a dangerous self-delusion. The
belief that the problem of poverty will die out as an issue in
the seventies was summarized for me recently by a white
professional man, actually a man of some compassion and
erudition, but with an unbelievably distorted cosmology.
Said he:

> The poor will always be with us, the Bible tells us, and I don't
> see how that harsh reality can be denied. I have seen poverty
> in Asia and South America which would make today's city
> ghetto-dweller seem like a king by contrast. There seems to be
> a natural ordering in which some will excel and others will
> have less in talent and rewards. While individuals of excel-
> lence will certainly arise from Negro ranks, most won't be-
> cause of genetic or natural laws.

Such a viewpoint as a general philosophy dulls the will
to act, and makes more certain the natural disastrous consequence of inaction.

As black incomes have grown along with white, the rise

27

s blacks has been matched by a *decline*
poor blacks. The words of the old song,
her and the poor get poorer" describe what
n the ghetto. The gap between black and
incomes has increased by over $900 since
ue that the poor in this country, white or black,
wealthy in many locations in the world; but it is
th   unding community that provides our standard and
measures our relative deprivation and our direction of
movement. In view of a rising tide of expectations, abstract
generalizations or obvious but irrelevant facts won't make
the problem go away. Poverty is the condition of about
30 million people in the United States, of whom 9 million
are black, according to reports by the Social Security Administration. (Poverty is defined as an income under $3,335
for an urban family of four.)

In urban areas, 41.7 percent of blacks live in poverty.
This poverty is twice as prevalent among families without a
male head. Add a child or children under six and poverty
among these families goes up to 81 percent. A majority of
the poor children in cities are black. Here is material for a
future explosion.

The Declining Quality of Life in the Slum

A fast-growing black population, mainly younger than
the white population, clustered in cities, without jobs, leads

to a quality of life which generates riots. Will the riots simply go away?

Many conservative writers and speakers have stressed the need for respect for law and order, which is certainly a necessity for a stable business environment. Yet, where do people learn to respect law and order? By getting a shot from a can of Mace? From a stoner gun slug? From a billy on their skull? Unfortunately when these confrontations occur the lesson is already six to twelve years too late. The crucial 20 percent of our population under ten years of age are already forming and reinforcing their opinion of law and order. They learned it in the slums of Harlem, Cork-town, Madison Street, Bedford-Stuyvesant, and the like. What's the quality of life there from which they draw their values?

1. The father has left home because of unemployment. In some cases he *must* leave for the mother to obtain certain kinds of relief payments. (The desire to receive Aid to Dependent Children of Unemployed, for example, has been noted as a positive motivation for formation of households headed by females.) When male unemployment exists in the same house where the female head is employed, the chances are very high that the husband will leave.

2. Since the father is gone and the mother works, the children are left to shift for themselves much of the time. Over 60 percent of black women work, and in some urban slums the proportion runs higher than that. Where are the kids, and what are they learning? The raw statistics of crime, illegitimacy, venereal disease, dope addiction, lack of sanitary conveniences, gambling, and every other imag-

29

inable evidence of social disintegration surround the youngster, who spends his days and nights on the street. Eleven percent of the children of Harlem were convicted of juvenile delinquency in 1965 (and these were the ones who were caught). Venereal disease among children under 21 ran at 1,600 per 100,000 reported cases the same year in black neighborhoods. Undetermined numbers estimated in the tens of thousands in New York City and Chicago are youngsters under 16 without an official place of residence. In Chicago major crimes, which include homicide, rape, aggravated assault, robbery, burglary, grand larceny, and auto theft, ran at a rate of 5,450 per 100,000 of population in the poorest black districts. Crimes against persons made up a majority of these. One low-income black district had 35 times as many crimes as did a high-income white district. The ratio clearly shows that the lower the income, the higher the crime rate, despite the assignment of more than four times as many patrolmen to these low-income areas. Eighty-five percent of the victims are black. Young blacks in the 14 to 24 age group commit the majority of the crimes. With the coming rise in the percentage of young people entering this age bracket, a sharp increase in crime may be expected. Health conditions are far worse than average in the slum areas. Unemployment, crowded conditions, substandard housing, and poverty produce a high incidence of serious diseases among black slum dwellers and high admissions to mental hospitals. Fewer health services, group medical insurance coverages, and sanitation and building maintenance services are available. Rats (and rat-bites upon children) are ordinary in the black slum.

30

Julius Horowitz, the novelist, describes in *The W.A.S.P.* the early life of a black boy, Ralph Mills. Born without knowing his father, "by the age of three he had seen more filth than eighty percent of the people . . . will ever see."

This is where 20 percent of our youngsters under ten are learning to respect law and order. It should seem obvious that the problem won't go away by itself.

The Rising Tide of Expectations

The fact that riots occur isn't explained by the people at the lowest level, the so-called "dregs," who in fact are not rioters, but accept life in the ghetto with apathy. The rioter, as we've seen, is the black who has risen just high enough from the bottom to have raised his aspirations. The underemployed has tasted the benefits of income, and his TV and his personal exposure to income and employment have led him to organize and fight for more. The specter of sliding back into the squalor and apathy of the worst-off, coupled with an increasing pride in race and color, has stiffened his spine.

No, Mr. Corporation Manager, here is a problem you can't solve by waiting it out. We must look for other solutions.

3

CAN GOVERNMENT SOLVE THE PROBLEM?

I saw that the state was half-witted, that
it was timid as a lone woman with her
silver spoons, and that it did not know its
friends from its foes, and I lost all respect
for it. Thus the state never confronts a
man's sense, intellectual or moral, but
only his body, his senses. It is not born
with superior wit or honesty, but with
superior physical strength.

Henry Thoreau,
ON CIVIL DISOBEDIENCE

Agreed that we have a problem, one that will not go away
of its own accord, can the corporation and its managers
shrug it off and leave it to the government? Certainly there
has been no shortage of governmental programs at all levels, and there is a role for government to play, mainly to get
out of the way when the solution is planned and under way.

Federal Programs

Ever since the turn of the century, when Theodore Roosevelt began his administration, we have seen a continual
stream of federal welfare programs designed to eradicate

poverty and injustice. In the face of the black revolt since 1964, new attacks upon unemployment and poverty have absorbed billions of dollars and millions of manhours.

Table 2 shows the costs of these governmental programs in 1968 and in part indicates the diversity of approaches employed and relative expense. Some of these cannot have any payoff in immediate employment, but tackle the problems of the young people who are already caught in the trap of poverty. Head Start, for 616,533 preschoolers, or child and infant health programs for 170,000 children, might, for example, have an almost immediate benefit. Others are subject to a scrutiny in terms of cost, if not effectiveness. The concentrated employment program designed to help 94,000 hard-core unemployed in slums in March 1967 was somewhat less than 10 percent successful. Renewed in cooperation with the National Alliance of Businessmen in January 1968, it has led to 100,000 new placements of unemployed blacks in private jobs. Other programs have often set their sights higher than is realistic, and unit costs for helping people have been far more than projected. In addition to this poor cost-effectiveness performance, duplication and excessive administration costs are rising faster than managerial capacity to handle them. Competition among the OEO (Office of Economic Opportunity), HEW (Health, Education, and Welfare), HUD (Housing and Urban Development) and others is also apparent. In more candid moments officials admit to this proliferation of programs, stating that it is easier to get several smaller projects through Congress, using several committees, than to shove through one giant poverty plan. Lastly, gross dishonesty, such as that uncovered in New York City programs, has greatly diminished the over-all effectiveness.

Table 2
Federal Program for the Poor
Fiscal Year 1968
(millions of dollars)

MAJOR PROGRAMS	SPENDING	WHERE THE MONEY GOES
I *Cash benefits* Social Security (HEW)	$ 7,900	Old-age and disability payments to an estimated 7.3 million poor
Public assistance (HEW)	3,500	Grants to 8.2 million under state welfare programs
Total	$11,400	
II *Health* Health insurance for aged (HEW)	$ 1,700	Medicare coverage for 6.3 million poor
Medical care (HEW)	1,400	Medicaid for 6.9 million welfare recipients and other poor
Vocational rehabilitation (HEW)	280	Diagnoses, treatment, services, and facilities for 697,500 poor
Indian health (HEW)	99	Furnishes health care, education to 390,000 Indians, Eskimos
Child and infant health (HEW)	56	Furnishes care for 170,000 children, 75,000 mothers
Comprehensive health services (OEO)	33	Neighborhood centers help 223,000
Total	$ 3,568	
III *Housing* Low-rent public housing (HUD)	$ 184	Helps finance 1.2 million poor people in 477,119 housing units
Neighborhood facilities (HUD)	27	Grants to build or rehabilitate about 100 community centers
Rent supplement (HUD)	4	Subsidizes 12,000 poor families or individuals in 3,350 units
Total	$ 215	

34

Table 2—Federal Program for the Poor—*continued*

MAJOR PROGRAMS	SPENDING	WHERE THE MONEY GOES
IV *Training and education*		
Precollege education (HEW)	$ 1,200	9.5 million students, 30% black
Head Start (OEO)	325	Preschool help for 616,533 children
Job Corps (OEO)	285	Training, education for 98,000 school drop-outs, 58% black
Neighborhood Youth Corps (OEO)	281	Jobs, training, education for 389,200 youths, 42% black
Manpower development (Labor Dept.)	251	Classroom and job training for 179,000, 48% and 32% black
College work-study grants (HEW)	102	Subsidizes part-time work for 226,300 needy students
Educational opportunity grants (HEW)	95	Grants to 170,412 poor college students
Concentrated employment (Labor Dept., OEO)	55	Helps 94,000 hard-core unemployed, 85% black, in 76 slums
Work incentive & training (HEW)	40	Trains or educates 32,000 welfare recipients for work
Upward bound (OEO)	30	Precollege help for 23,000
Vista (OEO)	30	Trains, pays 5,000 volunteers to work on 450 projects among poor
Migrants (OEO)	25	Education, housing, day care for 148,500 seasonal workers
Follow through (OEO)	15	Extra care in first school years
Total	$ 2,734	

Source: "The Rising Cost of Poverty Programs," *Business Week,* May 4, 1968, and Bureau of the Budget data.

The most important programs from our viewpoint are those which get people into employment, for it is in this area that the corporation must make its mark. It would not be especially useful to discuss all 25 of the programs displayed. Perhaps Table 2 is the best evidence of the plethora of approaches and the ingenuity of government officials in inventing new ways of job creation for middle-class social workers, economists, administrators, and the like. The success of these direct employment programs leaves much to be desired, however. To comment on a few of the major ones since 1960:

Area Redevelopment. This was a pr)gram designed to spread prosperity more evenly over paits of the economy, thus alleviating the effects of unemployment on the depressed or distressed areas. If unemployment rose disproportionately in Wilkes-Barre, the town received special assistance in the form of defense contract assignment, and special programs which would bolster its sagging economy. The program lacked teeth to force factories to move into the depressed areas (as Britain does), and its effects were relatively insignificant in terms of finding jobs for minority groups, since most such groups lived in areas where high levels of employment existed for everyone but blacks.

Manpower Development and Training Act. The mechanics and operational details of the MDTA are not all bad. It falls short for the most part because it started out with some totally erroneous and shortsighted assumptions on the part of Secretary of Labor Arthur N. Goldberg. Goldberg found many of these preconceptions reinforced during his visit to Sweden in the early 1960s.

His basic assumption was that *the rise of technology* had

left the uneducated or undereducated unemployable. The term "structural unemployment" caught on. A few think-tank teams developed a model which explained unemployment. Economist Charles Killingsworth of Michigan State University demonstrated that automation led to unemployment. This unemployment, others suggested, was the cause of low income, and low income by definition of the Social Security Administration was poverty. The reason automation caused unemployment wasn't simply that it destroyed jobs, since clearly it created high-level technical jobs which were in search of manpower. The reason the unemployed were in this lamentable condition was that they had insufficient education. The solution then, as Mr. Goldberg discovered it, was intensive training of the unemployed in reading, shop mathematics, shop skills, and the like. Once trained they would be qualified for the bright new technological world, and unemployment could be ended.

The educational establishment, from the public school systems up through the superstructure to HEW at the federal government level, grasped this idea eagerly. After all, if the educational system had a grip on the key to jobs, as it boldly declared in radio and TV spots, its product would be in great demand. "Drop-outs" became the subject of special attention. If a few wondered what was wrong in a system which lost 40 percent of its subjects before they completed the production line operation which was prescribed for them, they seldom focused upon the real problem: Does everyone really need all that education in order to be employed?

37

The model for the explanation of the MDTA would look something like Figure 1.

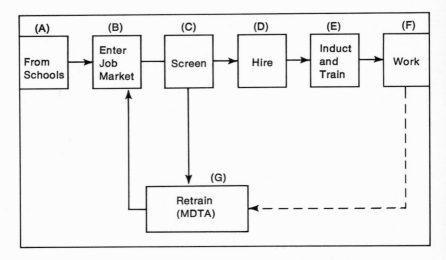

The youths emerging from the school system (A), by whatever door, at whatever stage, would enter the job market (B) in search of employment. At this point they would run into a screening process (C). The individual who qualified would move horizontally into being hired by an employer (D), who would induct and train him (E) in specific job requirements. After this he would go to work (F). MDTA entered the scene at two points. The first would be if the individual didn't have the qualifications to pass the first screen. He could enroll in a retraining course (G) to learn typing, practical nursing, retail sales, comptometer operations, and so on. This, of course, could only be done under the law if: (1) the person had the qualifications for learning (could pass some kind of aptitude test) or (2) if there was a known job opening available in that newly acquired skill after the training was completed. These two necessary conditions were a one-two punch knockout to many people, who would subsequently be left behind in the ghetto. Most couldn't pass any test.

The second place where MDTA entered, and showed some promise, was in the retraining of underemployed, those already holding jobs who desired to enlarge their skills and move upward by reentering the job market at a higher level. While this worked well for the hundreds of thousands who went through its programs, the great bulk of the people who comprised the slum problem were left essentially untouched. In other words, MDTA didn't do anything to get at the basic problem of unemployability, which also equaled untrainability. Many rejects weren't able to pass the screen because they didn't fit the MDTA criteria for eligibility for training. The reasons were often deeper.

Those administering the program recognized that it was not operating effectively. Those who hit the reject button were obviously in need of some diagnosis to determine the cause of their lack of qualifications, or even their lack of qualifications to learn how to become qualified. At this point remedial programs sponsored by OEO, HEW, and others flowered. These extended in area from reading skill deficiency, illiteracy, and physical limitations (need for glasses, for example) to apparent neuropsychiatric defects.

This approach, usually at a "demonstration project"

39

level, proved a quagmire of middle-class professors, social workers, and educationists, all running about shouting "Manpower!" The ultimate in success was if your project made such a splash that it was actually written up in the *Reader's Digest* or the new, socially aware *Look* magazine. The amazing ability of government agencies to waste money was once more proven, without any appreciable effect. The Job Corps took youngsters out of the slums and put them in discarded army camps, to the chagrin of neighboring cities. Neighborhood Youth Corps, Operation Acronym, and other such programs were all removed from the mainstream of life where the problem must be met.

Badly understaffed juvenile courts, with judges hearing as many as thirty-five cases a day, and performing the roles of judge, prosecutor, defense attorney, and guardian of the child, fought their dockets without any added funds for operations. Others could get a million dollars to study their functioning in a theoretical, evaluative, and experimental way without trouble.

Middle-class welfare workers, armed with master's degrees in social work, chased their own tails, uttering their foolish jargon, impervious to the human problem that stared them in the face, helpless to do a single constructive thing about it. The remedial programs after MDTA dumped millions into the morass of demonstration projects. Most projects were experimental studies performed by a profession which roved the ghetto streets naked, with paper sacks over their heads, repeating again and again, "We will save you, we will save you," yet utterly incapable of saving even themselves.

40

The United States Employment Service. Vital to the mechanical operation of the fruitless system was the USES (U.S. Employment Service, Department of Labor), with its operating arms in the states. Long considered by employers an informal internal arm of organized labor in government, it reflected the rising conservatism of the unions themselves. Under Secretary of Labor Willard Wirtz USES was often seen more as an instrument to protect union members from job competition than to find creative solutions to the problems of the hard-core unemployed. In return the labor movement rushed to protect the Labor Department from being merged with the Commerce Department. A brief burst of hope occurred during the period when Daniel Moynihan was Assistant Secretary, but in time the solid gray old guard, entrenched like feudal barons in the bureaus, fended off any attempts to change the Department's traditional objectives, as in house lobby for unions. The more brilliant and insightful younger staffers found themselves balked in obtaining action from the occupants of the key positions in the regional offices and in the dusty old building on Fourteenth Street, N.W., in Washington. As a department required to enforce wage, hour, and similar policing laws, they were unable to persuade many employers even to divulge accurate figures, for fear that they might be used as a club in a subsequent hearing on another matter. Labor Department officials were unsure how unemployment insurance differed from Social Security in administration; unsure how the OEO, as a White House darling, related to its Neighborhood Youth Corps; unsure of how the county agent of agricultural extension related to its

Farm Labor Service, made jittery by the EEOC (Equal Employment Opportunity Commission) Title VII program, which made the Women's Bureau of the Labor Department redundant; apprehensive about how Labor's ineffective Bureau of Apprenticeship related to the many OEO and HEW programs. Small wonder that the cafeteria and executive dining room at the Fourteenth Street Labor Department headquarters often heard speculation about whether the whole department might not be eliminated. President Johnson verified these fears when he tentatively proposed that Labor and Commerce be combined into a single department in 1966. Frantic lobbying by influential staffers and union chiefs with their favorite connection on Capitol Hill stifled the proposal for the moment, but didn't kill the idea.

Meanwhile employers used the state employment testing service to screen applicants, thus avoiding charges of racial bias in the handling of applicants. After all, if one government agency applied tests which actually resulted in *de facto* discriminatory hiring, could another file charges against the employer for job bias? The policy was antidiscrimination; the effect of testing for "qualifications" rejected blacks.

Uncle Sam Is a Bigot

Perhaps a more sardonic aspect of the government as a solver of the problem lies in its own record as an employer.

42

Despite the Executive Order of September 24, 1965, which declares "a positive continuing program in each executive department and agency" to achieve equal employment opportunity, in 1966 only 320 thousand of 213 million classified civil servants were black. Eighty-eight percent of the blacks were in the lowest-paying jobs, and they occupied less than two percent of the seven highest classifications of federal employees. As Julius Hobson pointed out in a recent article,

> In Washington, D.C., a city 64% black, where the federal government employs close to half the city's job holders, the FCC had managed never to hire a single black programmer. And this single federal agency managed to spend $24,000 on two years of hearings to block a black man from moving up one grade from his $4,776-a-year job. Eventually he was transferred to another agency without his promotion.[1]

Study of Minority Group Employment in Federal Government. In 1966 this study was issued by the Civil Service Commission. According to the study, white employees held four out of every five jobs in federal government in the nation's capital. Half of the employed blacks were in the bottom four grades and nine out of ten were in the bottom eight grades. Several agencies had no blacks in the grades known in government terminology as "GS rating" from GS 11 to GS 18. The Department of Health, Education, and Welfare, with over 70,000 employees, showed only five employees in the highest three grades. Hobson himself, an activist and an author of obvious verbal facility, was appraised badly by bosses who charged him with "lacking

43

self-confidence" and "inadequate command of English."
As he summarized his position:

> It seems unlikely that the Federal Government will take the
> necessary steps to carry out the President's order. As it now
> stands, Uncle Sam's self-policing, through the current crop of
> Equal Employment Opportunity officers, is tantamount to put-
> ting billy goats in charge of the garden. It's time the Federal
> Government ended its self-righteous hypocrisy. If it seriously
> intends to enforce its own laws, it had better start by enforcing
> them in its own house.[2]

Similar patterns of employment could be found wherever
government is the employer. The Civil Service, which was
designed to prevent discrimination by political patronage,
proves to be a suitable instrument of discrimination against
hiring the unemployed and upgrading the underemployed.

The key here of course lies in the determination that
"testing as usual" shall prevail. The assumptions are the
same as the qualification rationale of MDTA. It is educational system-oriented, and degrees are considered more
relevant than the results sought. The end effect is a middle-
class bias.

Is it likely, then, that a government which cannot manage
its own internal affairs can solve the problem for private
employers? Muscle it can employ. To private employers
the viewpoint is one of sanctimonious, humorless, and offi-
cious policing of the Presidential order with respect to government contractors, conducted by an organization that
resists movement away from a strong pro-white bias at the
pace of a tortoise with the gout.

The grand fallacy in "testing as usual" we'll look at later. The plain facts are that federal, state, local, and private employers have all established artificially high standards of employment. The emphasis upon "get qualified and you will be hired" must be reversed to become "we'll hire you and qualify you." The alternative is chaos.

What Is the Cost of Poverty Programs?

Federal spending for the poor only scratches the surface with the OEO appropriation of $2.2 billion. Howls of anguish often arise when civil rights advocates such as A. Philip Randolph, black chief of the Pullman Porter's union, suggests that the government should appropriate $50 billion a year for the cities and the urban crisis. This isn't at all unrealistic, nor beyond the realm of possibility. Table 3 shows the growth of federal spending for the poor in the period 1964–69. Most businessmen will not decry the cost, if it

Table 3
Federal Spending for the Poor, 1964–69
(billions of dollars)

YEAR	AMOUNT SPENT
1964	$13.4
1965	15.0
1966	18.3
1967	21.6
1968	24.6
1969	27.7 (est.)

Source: Constructed from Bureau of the Budget data.

45

achieves what one executive described as the condition which from his viewpoint would be necessary:

> I wouldn't mind paying for effective programs, which had a goal and achieved it. I can't see taxing everybody to the hilt to cover the costs of uncoordinated, disorganized and experimental programs which provide grants for every harebrain in the country. Show me a smart program that helps the fellow who needs it in the slum and I'll mail my check willingly.

If the programs worked, it has been noted, and the hard-core unemployed became employed, within five years their tax income would return to the government the cost of upgrading them.

Since the requirements of government in solving the problem of the ghetto would be that it acquire flexibility, wit, and adaptability, qualities which it clearly demonstrates it lacks, it hardly seems a hopeful source of solution.

In matters of muscle the government clearly excels. Only a government can put down riots and insurrections once they occur. Only a government can pass laws and enforce them. Social innovation it cannot handle, except through some enforcement mechanism. This of course can produce significant social innovation, but only on those problems which lend themselves to the enforcement mechanism.

The greatest barrier to government programs lies in the high costs and monumental inefficiency when government gets out of its sphere of enforcement. Infusions of large sums of public money will attract willing recipients on campuses and in lesser government bodies. The tax toleration of the public to such expenditures is of course limited and possibly within sight already. Richard Nixon declared that he would reduce expenditures for the cities by $8 billion. If his administration follows his platform, the private employer may expect more responsibility for employing blacks to fall on the private sector.

If government had the means, the program, and the will to solve the problem more effectively than any other group in our society, it would be good business practice to give them the green light. Unfortunately they don't have any of these. Only the corporation, working cooperatively with government, has these means at its disposal.

4

IS RIOT CONTROL THE ANSWER?

Let me tell you, you let a couple million
people get out of work, you gonna have a
little ole revolution on your hands.
There's gonna be some burnin' and
shootin' sho nuff. Some folks gonna get
killed.

Former Governor George Wallace,
in THE SATURDAY EVENING POST

If letting the problem go away of its own accord won't work, and the government's solutions seem to be beyond our tax toleration, are we left with another alternative? Perhaps, we ask, the answer is in stiff antiriot measures? "Next time," reported Director of Police Dominick Spina of Newark, "we won't waste five hours begging people to go home peacefully. . . . The minute the first brick goes through a window we'll start making arrests. This time there won't be any fooling around."

Is this the solution to disorder? Can the business executive simply work at the local level to beef up his police force and insure that they have plans for calling in National Guard and federal troops when disorder erupts? Is this an alternative to "hire 'em," which we have suggested is inescapable for the corporation?

48

The thesis of this chapter is that riot control is merely a necessary stopgap once the riots have broken out. Law enforcement agencies clearly must have the strength necessary to control immediate riots and anarchy. As anything approaching a long-run or even interim solution, riot control is harmful, however, in that it may give us a false sense of security, a belief that putting down riots will contain the problem.

The Military Learns from 1967

The performance of the riot control forces, including police and National Guard, during the 1967 riots was poor. The police were unequipped to deploy in military formations. Their command organization was aimed at deploying men in ones and twos over wide areas rather than in troop formations. They had little or no training in mass maneuvers and the tactics of mob control.

The various National Guard units were likewise unprepared by training and equipment, and they panicked easily. Too often they unlimbered .30 caliber rifles and blazed away, hitting innocent victims. With demands upon young civilian soldiers to act as patrolmen one instant and mob control units the next, the guards reacted badly.

Conferences since 1967 have helped amend many of these shortcomings. Better intelligence about the "enemy" plans, coupled with extensive training in summer camps of

49

the National Guards around the nation, prepared police and National Guard for the disruptions which were anticipated for 1968. The four to five days of rioting following the assassination of Martin Luther King, Jr. provided large-scale maneuvers under fire for many of them.

Speed of response, tight curfews during the night hours, and being slower on the trigger in shooting looters seems to be the strategy. At Fort Gordon, Ga. and Fort Belvoir, Va., federal troops have undergone by Presidential order thirty hours of riot training instead of the two hours previously provided. Better weapons, superior communications equipment, intelligence agents among the civil rights activists, and better coordination between local, state, and federal units are part of the preparation to put down disorders.

New weapons or devices in the riot control armory, including tear gas, shotguns, and a new Stoner Rifle which can fire a slug through a brick wall, are part of the apparatus of control. Helmets and bulletproof vests are selling well among police departments of the nation. Some state police have purchased armored cars.

One of the key issues is when to shoot and when not to shoot. Faced with a mob, the tactical troops, police, or Guards pitch tear gas and move forward toward the mob. If the crowd runs they are allowed to escape. If they fight, they are arrested.

Looting and firebombing have been another matter of debate. Mayor Richard Daley of Chicago aroused howls of anger from civil rights groups and others when he growled that any arsonist would be shot. He later retracted some of

50

this statement. Police Chief Walter Headley of Miami took an even tougher line. Said he, "When the looting starts the shooting starts." Police Director Dominick Spina declares that his men will shoot only when the life of an officer or another person is threatened.

To find disabling substitutes for guns, many have taken recourse to Chemical MACE, an aerosol spray which causes tears, choking, and a burning sensation. The person hit goes down instantly and is out of action for twenty minutes or more. Many civil rights groups have declared MACE unsafe. Tests conducted by the University of Michigan proved it not harmful when used properly. "The trouble with that is that a scared cop isn't a scientist using it under the laboratory conditions of the test," declares Dr. Al Wheeler, president of the Michigan NAACP. Gun-propelled injections of tranquilizers such as forest rangers use on bears are too slow. Vinegar is believed by some to induce muscle spasm. RiotTrol is a slickening agent which when sprayed on a wet street or sidewalk causes the rioters to slip and slide.

With a police force armed and protected against mobs, the possibility is high that mass riots will not be the scheme of the future. Yet, riot control has a way of arousing counterstrategies among rioters. After all, as every moviegoer saw in *Dr. Zhivago,* mounted horsemen aligned from sidewalk to sidewalk can devastate a mob afoot. Yet, for the czars, putting down mob violence seemed to bring no permanent solution, only new and less controllable kinds of resistance.

The 1968 tactics work—the 1969 experience bears this out with respect to mob behavior—for containing black

51

mobs to their own areas and for barring them from white residential and commercial areas. This becomes necessary to avoid the unleashing of opposing mobs of whites, who have been relatively quiet to date, but who have been buying weapons at an unprecedented rate. Should blacks break the barriers and rush into white sectors, it is to be expected that white mobs would retaliate, and police would be battling both blacks and whites.

The Safe Streets and Crime Control Act of 1968

In February 1967 President Johnson submitted a proposal to Congress for a law to control violence in the streets, curb ownership of guns by citizens, and achieve law and order. This last purpose, much beloved of conservative columnists, is presumably to be achieved through the final version of the Johnson proposal, which he signed into law in June 1968. The law was somewhat altered in its passage through Congress, and he muttered briefly about vetoing it because of its shortcomings, but the Senate majority leader himself was reported to have declared that Johnson's veto would be overridden, so he signed it.

It provides $400 million for a two-year improvement program for local police forces, which now expend $2.5 billion. Title I of the act provides that the emphasis in spending this money must be upon riot control, and not for ordinary crime prevention. The act also opens the practice of wiretapping somewhat, a fact which disturbs some. Despite a flood of mail pressing for tighter gun control, the act really didn't effectuate the desires popularly expressed. Although two of the larger gun manufacturers had stated that they did not oppose gun control, the law nonetheless provided rather limited procedures to control weapons in the hands of the public. A controversial wiretapping provision gives a forty-eight-hour opening for police forces in cases where an emergency exists, with the judgment as to what constitutes an emergency being placed largely in the hands of the police official involved. President Johnson was apparently made uneasy by this and cautioned against our becoming a "nation of snoopers bending to the keyholes of homes and offices of America."

While the riots of 1967 and 1968 were clearly before the Congress, the assassinations of President John F. Kennedy and Senator Robert Kennedy were apparently uppermost in the reasons behind the gun control legislation, for that Title dealt mainly with barring mail-order guns, sales to minors of hand guns, and sales of hand guns to out-of-state residents. Ammunition sales are subject to the same restrictions.

While the emphasis in the Safe Streets Act is mainly upon the index crimes of assault, forcible rape, murder, and the like, the provisions are closely related to the recommendations of the Kerner Commission. The concern of liberals with the law was expressed in the *New Republic's* editorial "Law and Order" at the end of June 1968:

> Even liberty may be surrendered in desperation, in exchange for the promise of safety. People flee from a freedom which is anarchy.

The control of crime is essentially control of crime in the ghetto, which is not unrelated to rioting and civil disorder. Even a better and tighter law to achieve safe streets will not bring about law and order if riots or guerrilla actions are a product of disbelief in the social order. The larger problems of social disorganization, the disintegration of the black family, and the belief of ghetto residents that the only recourse is to "get a gun" will not be solved by speeches and editorials on law and order, or even statutes which flick at the symptoms.

The Limitations of Riot Control

Given a specific mob on a specific street at a particular time, there's no doubt that the policeman or soldier, armed and trained, has the advantage. As Harold Martin has said,

Ceramic body armor, originally designed to protect helicopter crews fighting in Vietnam, is now available to police, as are hand-held shields like those once worn by Caesar's centurions. Wearing a helmet that will turn a bullet, a visor to protect his eyes, shin guards, an aluminum athletic supporter and shoes with steel protective plates in the toes, the modern police officer goes on riot duty padded like a hockey goalie and looking like a man from Mars.[1]

Well protected against most kinds of mob weaponry, and directed by an alerted and prepared command organization, the policeman or soldier can hardly lose. Won't this do the trick, then? Perhaps the whole mob can be bottled up and kicked senseless as a movement, and corporations therefore won't have to do anything?

William Day, president of Michigan Bell Telephone and a member of the New Detroit Committee, a citizens' group formed to alleviate the causes of riots, once made this observation about the blacks in the civil rights movement: "One thing I've learned, these people aren't stupid." This being true, it is highly unlikely that they will continue to repeat the same tactics for which the police and army are preparing countermovements. The most logical development beyond mass action, the burning and looting of entire blocks as in the Madison Street riot in Chicago, would be guerrilla warfare.

There are other weaknesses in riot control, contained within the ranks of the riot control troops themselves. Should the militant black group persist in rioting and other forms of violent resistance and rebellion, the very steadfastness of troops themselves would be subject to some question. Apart from the fact that many of them are black, it is well known that neither police nor Guards relish sustained combat with unarmed people, especially when they are of their own nationality or race. During the 1968 student and worker riots in Paris, when the government of General DeGaulle was threatened, he slipped out of Paris to consult with his generals. After he had met with General Jacques Massau, it was reported that the generals would back their leader in the event of revolution, but "would not fire on students or workers." The possibility that his generals might not back his hand, in short would mutiny, was realized by the canny leader, and was the reason for his checking them to begin with.

Persistent and widespread racial violence, with troops pitted against mobs armed with makeshift or stolen weapons, plus a military which is reluctant to fight civilians in a mass way, is the mixture that produces genocide. The purpose of the gas chambers in Nazi Germany was not merely a drive for Teutonic efficiency. As Rudolf Hoess, the commandant at Auschwitz, reported in his autobiography, it was "consideration for the troops," who were being ordered to conduct mass executions by rifle, that led to more efficient methods. Apparently the command to shoot helpless people created tensions even among hardened SS troopers. Gas chambers and genocide may seem an original and shocking topic here, but it is not as uncommon a subject in our society as one might suppose. In 1964 I sat in the faculty club of one of the nation's leading universities and heard a distinguished professor emeritus declare in all seriousness that the Cleveland riots of the day before merely indicated that ultimately "this country will need an Eichmann for the final solution of the nigger problem." The widespread support of racists is symptomatic of an appalling range of possibilities.

The real problem isn't one of what the country, the liberals, the right-thinking people should do about a governor who has stated: "That's why we don't have any of that business down here. They start a riot down here, first one of 'em to pick up a brick gets a bullet in the brain, that's all." The really important question is: What was there about George Wallace's behavior that got him elected governor in Alabama, and more cogently, why did his racism and near-genocidal pronouncements make him an important candidate for President of the United States in the North? For most of us, to be as coldly analytical as a RAND Corporation behavioral scientist working on a megadeath model is impossible. However, we might observe, in the context of this book for hard-nosed businessmen, that it would also be bad for business, if you are really concerned. Along with Jews, there were numerous political prisoners, and numerous businessmen, put into concentration camps for such major crimes as price-fixing and similar practices for which lesser remedies now exist. Genocide as a logical development from continued rioting and its uncontrolled development may seem remote. It is not implausible to speculate about it, however, nor is it astronomically improbable. Given a well-organized clustering of units such as the Blackstone Rangers and the like and a few striking victories of the mob over the troops, and the same panic that produced the evacuation of the Japanese from the West Coast in World War II would seem perfectly possible. This is hardly an option to relish when another alternative exists.

Transition to Guerrilla Warfare

In all likelihood, while the police and military have been adapting tactics and weapons based upon lessons from past battles, black leadership has been cogitating upon alternative strategies. The most probable of these would be

57

guerrilla warfare, the lessons of 1968 reveal. In many ways the conditions in the many ghettos are suitable for effective guerrilla warfare. As the noted German military theorist Carl Von Clausewitz set them forth in 1832, for effective guerrilla action there must be five conditions:

1. The war must be carried on in the interior of the country.
2. The war cannot hinge on a single battle.
3. The theater of war must extend over a considerable area.
4. The national character must support the war.
5. The country must be irregular, difficult, inaccessible.[3]

While Clausewitz was generalizing from Spanish guerrillas rising up against Napoleon, and from similar uprisings of national populations against invading armies, it doesn't take much imagination to apply the same principles to an armed minority in the center cities of the land. The key to guerrilla warfare is the small mobile unit. It must always be on the offensive, its actions being pinpricks, raids, and ambushes, with few if any last-ditch stands. Mao Tse-tung wrote, "The ability to run away is the very characteristic of the guerrilla."[4]

As Paret and Shy point out, much traditional guerrilla warfare was a defensive action by armed civilians against a foreign invader. In this century, and in this decade, the function has often changed from defensive to insurrectionary and offensive. Clearly guerrilla warfare is not the tool for the large power, with its divisions of troops, airmobile regiments, air forces and massive logistic support. Guerrilla warfare becomes a systematic tool of the disaffected minority for the seizure of power. The Bolshevik seizure of Russia, Mao's conquest of China, and Fidel Castro's capture of power in Cuba are examples of successful Communist efforts in our time. T. E. Lawrence's operations against Turkish communications during World War I in Arabia and the Jewish operations against the British and Arabs after 1945 are non-Communist examples.

Since the objectives of modern guerrilla warfare are both political and military, the structure of guerrilla forces requires military leadership matched equally by political and ideological leadership down to the lowest and smallest unit. The three major organizational units required are illustrated in Figure 2.

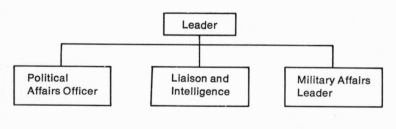

FIGURE 2.

To date, through the nonviolent approach, closely tied to Christian churches, the political, legal, and ideological sides have been well developed. The ideology of poverty and repression already exists. Liaison and intelligence can be obtained from newspapers and from contact with a population which has an underlying general sympathy with the cause. The ability to infiltrate military and police forces is

59

not beyond the realm of the possible. All that is missing is the military capacity, which for guerrillas is readily achieved among the 16- to 24-year-olds who have a rising pride of race, a deep sense of injustice, and the physical agility and bravado to serve as guerrillas.

Che Guevara pointed out that the guerrilla leader must be continually aggressive, but must never risk defeat.[5] The city as a base of operations, and a sizable population of blacks into which the guerrillas could dissolve, averts one of Guevara's problems, that of concealment, moving the guerrilla away from supplies, suitable targets, and civilian leaders who could be won to their cause. The next danger to guerrilla movement which Guevara noted is the damaging consequences upon others whose support is hoped for, but who are repelled by its ill effects upon them. The final problem of the guerrilla is determining when he has victory in his grasp. In the case of Castro this was the total capture of the society. For the urban black guerrilla the objective would be much less clear. The ultimate outcome must be a political concession, such as was sought by the Poor People's March on Washington in 1968, with the encampment in Resurrection City. As a nonviolent protest it was purely political. Because the goals were unclear, and the execution was mismanaged, it achieved little except some promises of further study by Cabinet-rank officers who hoped to avoid embarrassment of the administration and the party in power in an election year.

Given the unclear purposes which would be inherent in black guerrilla actions, the chances are high that it would merely produce a protracted state of terrorism, dragging

60

on interminably much like the Algerian terrorism, until either counterguerrillas sapped away its strength, or some token gesture of capitulation could be worked out at the political level.

An American Algeria would undoubtedly generate sufficient public resentment among middle-class blacks and whites and among a suffering ghetto population that panic reactions of a fairly extensive nature, approaching relocation or genocide, would probably ensue.

What Does It All Add Up To?

Why this horror story, dragging out the possibilities for full inspection this way? Refer to the Preface. The assumption is that I have made a statement, "Corporations must do wholesale hiring of blacks" and we are exploring your possible alternatives, as a businessman.

"But . . ."

Forget it; you have no choice as a corporation executive. Where there's a will there's a way. This book is aimed at your will. You'll find a way, and as a glimmer of hope, you'll find that it not only can be done, but can be done profitably.

> **Riot control when large groups of people are breaking the law is a must. If guerrilla warfare or terrorism erupts it must be put down. To see this as a total answer is to beg the question. The causes which produce the disorders must be eradicated. This eradication lies in jobs, lots of them, for ghetto dwellers. Only corporations can assume this responsibility.**

61

5

THE MILITARY SERVICES AS A POSSIBLE SOLUTION

Under the proper conditions Negro
veterans back from Vietnam could make
Rap Brown look like Little Lord
Fauntleroy.
Whitney Young, Jr.,
THE NEW YORK TIMES, March 24, 1968

In one form or another, the military services have cropped up from time to time as a possible vehicle for the solution of black unemployment. One group of managers, in discussing the problem of the urban crisis and its solution, posed the possibility that the necessity of maintaining an army and navy at vast expense might be utilized for another purpose: providing controlled and useful employment for otherwise unemployable black males. The moderator turned the question back to the group: "Would all of you who would relish a five-million-man all-Negro army please raise their hands?"

A nervous titter ran through the group, as it dawned upon them what the shocking consequences to "white security" might be of such a striking force, armed with modern weapons such as rockets.

At the same time, lesser levels of solution, using the existence of the military as a site of employment, and possible development and upgrading, have not gone without serious attention. Perhaps these could be the solution, rather than the one this book has persistently returned to: *"Corporations must hire the hard-core unemployed blacks."*

Several issues should be faced here:

- Is there room for these men in the military service?
- Would the solution alleviate the urban crisis?
- What would happen to the quality of the defense effort?
- What will be the impact of the black veteran?

The Impact of Military Manpower Policy

It is plain that the military has a concern for the manpower aspects of its recruiting and draft policies. Testifying in 1964 before the Senate Subcommittee on Employment and Manpower, the Clark Subcommittee, Norman S. Paul, Assistant Secretary of Defense for Manpower, stated:

As a very substantial employer of manpower during periods of national emergency, the Department of Defense shares a common interest in the effective education and training of our youth and in combating the wastage of human skills resulting from unemployment.[1]

63

Over three million men are in the regular military establishment, and another million participate regularly in training in the reserves and the National Guard. This runs in the range of five percent of the nation's labor force. Military service could solve the problem of finding employment for the hard-core black unemployed if enough of them could be inducted to blunt the disorders by getting them off the streets into roles where they could be trained and managed.

This, of course, would presume erroneously that every job in the military is one which could be done by the lowest skill level available, and also presumes that we could make the draft legally amenable to such a discriminatory practice.

The trend in military occupations since the end of World War II has been in technical directions. Today over 1,500 specialist occupations exist in all services. There are, for example, as many electronics specialists as there are foot soldiers.

There are more clerks than foot soldiers (Table 4). The mechanic and the technician make up more than a third of all military manpower.[2] Although the Vietnam War altered

Table 4
Enlisted Occupations

	PERCENT
Electronics	14.4
Mechanics	32.5
Craft and service	18.1
Clerical	18.8
Ground combat	14.2

Source: Clark Subcommittee, 1964.

these figures somewhat because of the commitment of more foot soldiers, the basic percentage relationship remains at about these levels. As Table 5 indicates, in 1963

Table 5
Military Service Status of Males 18½–26½ Years Old

	PERCENT
Entered service	37.2
Unfit for service	32.9
Deferred	22.7
Pool	7.2

Source: Clark Subcommittee, 1964.

about one-third of the total male population between 18½ and 26½ years was listed as "unfit for service." They were generally unfit for service by criteria which are the *same* criteria that make them unemployable in corporations by ordinary standards. This could be because they have criminal records, are illiterate, have been committed in the past to mental institutions, do not meet the minimum physical requirements, or cannot pass standard mental or psychiatric examinations.

The demands of national security for a certain personal and performance level, the military manpower planners declare, would indicate that there is "no room for the career private." The Vietnam War enlarged the demand for them in combat positions. Where such posts exist they are ordinarily filled by recruits and trainees who fill them temporarily. If there is an oversupply in the ranks of the "unfit for service," occupants of the posts would be readily replaced. The key turnover problem of the military is among the higher specialists, such as the electronics technician, whose service-acquired skills are salable on the civilian job market, and who therefore tend to leave.

All of this adds up to a pattern of discrimination in the military which leaves most ghetto youth on the streets. The Armed Forces Qualification Test has a minimum passing score of 10, which indicates the equivalent of a fifth-grade education. Persons below this level proved to be incapable of absorbing military instruction in technical tasks, and accounted for a majority of the disciplinary problems which arose. Following the acceleration of the Vietnam War, the standards were lowered through supplemental tests which qualified a larger number of the previously unfit. Beyond this, former Secretary of Defense Robert S. McNamara announced a program of opening the gates to 100,000 young men whose rejection had been most firm, with special remedial programs to correct many of the more correctable mental defects, such as illiteracy, and physical defects. Although it is rather early to come to a definite conclusion, the lessons for industry are worth noting. A significant number of this unfit group who were inducted have been upgraded and then proceeded to serve normal enlistments, including further training. Why, then, should corporations move in where the military is already doing the job?

The Black Soldier

The army has practiced a strict form of integration of units since the end of World War II, when the last of the segregated divisions and regiments was broken up. The

93rd Infantry Division, which served in the Pacific, and the 92nd in Italy, were disbanded as exclusively black divisions and their personnel scattered through the army at large. Black men made up about 10 percent of the men in uniform in 1968, but comprised 17 percent of the men assigned to combat positions. In some of the elite airborne units blacks comprise as much as 45 percent of the force. Of combat noncommissioned officers in Vietnam, about one in four is black. Of commissioned officers from Lieutenant to General about 5 percent are black, and these are mainly concentrated in the first three commissioned grades. About 66 percent of the blacks in the army reenlisted prior to 1968. In 1968 the proportion fell to 31 percent, but the rate is still three times the reenlistment rate among whites.

The price paid by black youth is disproportionately high. In the first five years in Vietnam over 20 percent of the casualties were black, even though the blacks represented only 12 percent of the total armed forces there. The black soldier is more apt to wind up in a combat outfit, and is more apt to be sent to Vietnam, where he is more likely than his white comrade to get hit. Of the 100,000 a year taken in under Secretary McNamara's "Project 100,000" 40 percent are black, and they are assigned to combat at an even higher rate than are black soldiers who qualify for service in the regular course of events. Daniel Moynihan, writing in *New Republic* in 1966, suggested that:

Very possibly the best hope is seriously using the armed forces as a socializing experience for the poor—until somehow their environment begins turning out equal citizens.

67

If the black man enters the Marine Corps under Project 100,000, the chances are over 87 to 100 that he will end up in combat. That he has been a good soldier has been testified by General William Westmoreland in a widely publicized 1967 speech before the South Carolina legislature.

While it is indisputable that for the black soldier to learn to read and write, be brought to good health, and have his teeth fixed, are all good things to have happen to him, there is little civilian application of the skills he acquires in the infantry except making his own bed, walking extensively, shining his own shoes, and *operating a rifle or machine gun with professional skill.*

It is the last item that is the source of concern to some observers, and in fact might be a persuasive argument for the corporation's assuming a major role in solving the urban crisis. This fact has been tacitly recognized by the military, which has solicited industry cooperation in Project Transition, which brings private industry onto military posts to conduct job-training programs for men with less than six months left to serve. Black men who have obtained no useful civilian skills while in service get preference in enrollment.

The Returning Veteran

An average of 40,000 blacks a month are discharged from the armed forces, about 5,000 of whom have been in combat zones. Every war, since the Revolutionary War, has seen a wave of civilian apprehension over the return of the killers. The stories and articles about "when Johnny comes marching home" extend from advice to lock up your daughters to the prediction that all the returning will become angry young men. Two recent stories, one in *The New York Times Magazine* by Sol Stern, an editor of *Ramparts* magazine, and another syndicated through the wire services to newspapers across the land, dealt with the ominous possibility of black veterans becoming militant.

Attempts to size up the dynamite in such a steady flow of returned combat veterans to the slums are usually pretty speculative. The *Times* story[3] reports on the case of Charles Cato, who spent a year in combat in Vietnam, and says, "I don't want to make any trouble." He can't find a job and is on unemployment, and lives in the Bedford-Stuyvesant section of Brooklyn. David Tuck of Cleveland, however, came back to his job at the post office and is angry about the war, the ghetto he came home to, and society in general. Other stories report similar extreme opposite positions. The plain facts are that nobody really knows what percentage of the returning blacks will behave militantly in the turbulent arena of the city and the ghetto.

On one hand, there is a theory that you have taken a poorly educated, poorly motivated young black man, run him through the military machine, given him no skills, and then returned him to society more disciplined and combat trained; and you now have a nascent terrorist or guerrilla.

On the other hand, combat experience has never created much of a desire for a further fight. As the two Bill

69

Mauldin characters on leave in World War II observed as they saw a jaunty young recruit strutting along the street of Naples, "He can't be a combat veteran, he's lookin' for a fight." Tired of fighting and killing, happy to be alive, trying to get back into the swing of civilian life, getting more schooling, finding a job, he is not prone to get too deep in civil rights activity and urban warfare. For one thing, the civilians who would like to enlist him in their cause are probably no more understanding of what he has been through, nor even willing to listen to his story, than any other civilian. There is a kind of apartness that separates men who have been in combat from those who haven't. The hidden presence of combat memories, shared with a now dispersed group, some dead, temporarily isolates him from those who never were there. It is far more likely that a man who counted socks in a Quartermaster depot, or served drinks in the officer's club in Fort Benjamin Harrison, will be an activist and militant than the ex-GI who actually was under fire. His killer instincts are more verbal than actual.

Black activists point freely to the high casualty rates among black soldiers as evidence of the racism of the white establishment. To Stokely Carmichael the facts are evidence that the white man is trying to eliminate the black people in the ghettos. To Carlos Russell, another black leftist leader, they comprise a combat pool for black insurrection in the ghetto if needed. "They have been trained to kill; if rebellions break out and they see their black brothers and sisters slaughtered by racist cops they will come to the defense of their own. They offer a good resource of skills

70

and technical know-how to those in the movement who feel that the only solution is armed struggle." Whitney Young, Jr. of the Urban League declares that "it would be realistic to expect such experts of mines and booby traps and other forms of destruction to find good reason why they should use these skills and risk their lives against the enemy of personal injustice as they did against the enemy of Communist aggression." Otilio Mighty of the Urban League adds that "if some of the vets use what they learned over there it won't really be surprising."

As a returning black Vietnam veteran from Ypsilanti, Mich., told this writer:

> I got a cold eye for anybody who tries to take me in on any deals whatsoever. Some of those black activist guys are real generous in committing the returning black vet to all-out fire-fights in the streets. I don't buy that any more than I would buy a recruiting sergeant conning me into another hitch in Vietnam. I want to see Carmichael and all those guys out front leading the charge before I mix it up. I'm bettin' that he'd be back in headquarters like the white generals were in Vietnam. I'm nobody's wind-up tin soldier anymore. But corner me where I gotta fight and I'll do as good as the next guy, and maybe a lot better than most of these guys who never seen combat.

Whatever his disposition to engage in activist movement in civilian life, the returning black veteran is a force to be reckoned with. Despite the civil rights leadership, he is not yet in their corner, armed and ready to be released. However, as Sol Stern concludes:

71

Ultimately it is extremely dangerous to try to use the military to solve social problems in a society that is torn by racial conflict. . . . A society that feeds millions of its disadvantaged young men into the military machine in the name of "civil rights" may only ensure that when racial conflict reaches its violent climax it will be fought on both sides with greater military sophistication and more lethal weapons by young men grown accustomed to killing.[4]

Partial Victory Equals Total Loss

It would seem that the use of the military as a solution— an alternative to corporations actively recruiting and hiring hard-core unemployed and unqualified people, then qualifying them—has some severe limitations. It could be a disastrous solution if it were not coupled with aggressive and skilled action by corporations.

Ultimately some specific percentage of returning black veterans might be enrolled in domestic conflict. If it were as high as one percent of the returning groups, they could lay waste a city and tie up its ordinary life for months through guerrilla tactics and terrorism. That there are already leaders who would be delighted to lead such a movement is no secret. The possibility of averting or minimizing this outcome lies in drawing out from under them the base they need for concealment, support, and sustenance. If the population by and large of the ghetto is well to do, steadily employed, and regularly building up personal stocks of goods, appliances, cars, and property, they will withhold such support. If, on the other hand, they are kept with 30 percent unemployment, with a majority living in poverty and seeing their kids growing up poor, they may silently cheer, and covertly slip support to the more aggressive among them.

Terror, coercion, and extortion, if they destroy the livelihood of the poor, produce a backlash that weakens and ultimately destroys them. The Communist guerrillas in Greece in 1946 were ultimately defeated because they drove the poor out of their territory into the cities. The Vietcong, in their Saigon campaigns, perhaps become a model for the black guerrilla in the American city. By fading into the ordinary environment during the day, even perhaps working as a loyal employee, he can emerge by night to terrorize. This blending into the environment can be accomplished only with the support of the population, as Mao points out.

A strong infusion of jobs, purchasing power, and prosperity into the potential areas of disorder has a beneficial effect. It produces a separation of the guerrilla and the terrorist from a base in the population.

The Black Militants

If the black veteran were to be organized, it would in all

73

likelihood be in some fashion related to the existing black militant organizations, such as the Black Panthers or the Blackstone Rangers. The Panthers, which originated in the South, are mainly a California group, based around Oakland, headed by Huey Newton, a Baptist minister's son. He was a street kid from early youth. After some law school, and being in and out of jail often, he teamed up with other militants to form a revolutionary party, adopting the panther symbol "because it is not the Panther's nature to attack anyone first, but when attacked and backed into a corner he will respond viciously."[5] Their early growth came out of a willingness to carry guns, a policy which made whites uneasy and aroused the Oakland police force to some drastic countermeasures. On one occasion they showed up at Sacramento for a meeting of the legislature and carried guns into the spectators' gallery. The furor was immense. The Panthers often were seen patrolling the Oakland ghetto in cars, guns prominently displayed, openly checking on the police. If a police car accosted a black man, the Panthers gathered around and advised the black man of his rights. They often were involved in actual violence, their revolutionary aims being centered upon the police, the white man's front-line force. In 1968 Newton was placed under grand jury indictment in connection with the shooting of an Oakland policeman, and became a cause of much protest activity in the black community.

As a self-professed revolutionary force, having their own Prime Minister (Stokely Carmichael) and Minister of Justice (Rap Brown), the Panthers would seem to meet the requirements of a militant group. The chance of their recruiting any significant number of ex-GI's appears slim. The rituals of raised fists, their colorful but odd-looking uniforms with black berets and black leather jackets, and their willingness to engage in spectacular maneuvers are most unlikely to appeal to the returning veteran.

The Blackstone Rangers are more like a large street-corner gang such as those publicized among whites in Brooklyn and lower New York after World War II. They lounge around pool halls and street corners on Chicago's South Side. White critics were enraged recently when the OEO granted $927,341 to the gang to provide basic education and job training for gang members.[6] Charges that they constitute a black Mafia are made by law enforcement officials. On the other hand, friends of the 800-man gang include a Presbyterian minister and, obviously, somebody in the federal poverty program.

The fact that a gang had received a grant from the OEO seemed somewhat anomalous to the Senate Permanent Investigating Subcommittee in July 1968, which invited a number of the people involved to Washington for a chat about the Blackstone Rangers. Despite some flurries of charges that the local Presbyterian Church kept marijuana and guns, the most relevant point here is that violence is apparently not foreign to the Rangers. A feud with the East Side Disciples, a rival gang, was reported by Chicago police to be the cause of 29 gang deaths in the Rangers' territory this year. The Senate Committee became a trifle exercised when Commander William Griffith of the Chicago police department, whose territory includes that of the Rangers, reported that following the OEO grant to the Rangers the number of killings jumped to 72 in the first six months after the grant, contrasted with a mere 42 prior to the grant. A number of South Side businessmen charged that the Rangers augmented their income from the federal government by selling protection against riots for prices reported at $125 a week.

Numerous other cities report similar gangs, following the two patterns exemplified by the Panthers on one hand and the Rangers on the other. Of the two it would seem that the revolutionary objectives of the Panthers would make them a more dangerous model, in terms of their potential for rebellion and terrorism along guerrilla lines. On the other hand, the Blackstone Rangers would, in all likelihood, be more comfortably traditional and less ideological, and therefore more attractive to the black veteran who couldn't find a job. The hometown of Al Capone can hardly see anything new.

The Conclusion

The corporation may find some active resistance and support in the existing programs of the military. It would be foolhardy to assume, however, that this is an alternative to employment of the hard-core black unemployed by business.

High levels of induction into military service require equally high levels of employment opportunity for the returning veteran with combat experience. To assume that military service will solve the urban crisis without such a corporate program will be productive of even more sophisticated violence in the cities, either in revolutionary gangs, in criminal gangs, or in spur-of-the-moment reaction by individual veterans.

6

CAN SOME NEW WAY BE DEVELOPED?

As long as you're up, get me a Grants.
Advertisement

One of the more striking aspects of the behavior of the academic community is that its dedication to knowledge seems to follow the sources of available money, as iron filings do a magnet. For a while the rush was for foreign countries as the Agency for International Development and other foreign programs provided funds for research into underdeveloped countries. Many a university such as MIT, the University of California, and Michigan, has erected barbed-wire fences around parts of its engineering research facility, and arranged *secret* security clearances for professors in order to tap the apparently inexhaustible funds of the defense establishment. Although many such grants seem less attractive when students riot in protest or when the humorless men from Washington come around later counting buildings to be sure the overhead charges were legitimate, the rush to the available funds is natural.

Since 1967 it has been apparent that the rate of growth of funds for physical and engineering research is sloping off rapidly. At the same time, the amount of money being spent for research into economics and the social sciences, and for demonstration grants relating to poverty, blacks, and the urban crisis has been rising rapidly. Undoubtedly, as one irreverent professor stated, "black is green."

The rising level of expenditure for the poor has produced a sum which, my estimates show, is about equal to that representing the cuts in physical research. The physical scientists have not, of course, been taking the cuts lying down. The screams of anguish and woeful statements by Presidential advisers on science and Nobel Prize winners ("Get Jerry, get Linus") have been impressive. Undoubtedly when a sharply rising curve begins to level off, weightlessness, if not mindlessness, is likely to emerge.

The lessons for the social and behavioral sciences are apparent. As Table 6 shows, when no crisis such as Sputnik

Table 6
U.S. Support for Research and Development
(billions of dollars)

	TOTAL	ACADEMIC
1956	3.5	0.25
1958	4.5	0.30
1960	8.0	0.45
1962	11.5	0.75
1964	15.5	1.05
1966	16.0	1.35
1968	16.5	1.40

Source: The New York Times, June 21, 1968.

exists the space program is cut back, and the physical branch of research suffers. The riots drew crisis-attention to the social sciences, and funds flowed in their direction as never before. When the Kerner Commission was formed it was instructed to find out and report on: What happened? Why did it happen? What can be done to prevent it from happening again?

This purpose obviously called for a kind of specialist who could deal with economics, statistics, field interview: in other words psychologists and other behavioral and social scientists. The descriptions of the rioters, interviews with rioters and nonrioters to learn their motives, and similar specific activities were competently carried out. Rather than pursuing their custom of studying some trivial matter of interest to practically nobody, the social science-trained staff, including lawyers, performed superbly because they were working on a real problem with some specific objectives and a time urgency. Such a pattern of behavior, if continued, could be the making of the social scientist.

Unfortunately, the expenditures of research money under demonstration grants and small research projects, apart from certain task-oriented chores that were assigned, have produced little if anything that promises a solution which would let a reluctant businessman off the hook. The evidence still points, as will be seen, toward the corporation as the last, best hope of solving the urban crisis.

The Poverty Research Industry

The literature describing research on poverty has become so voluminous as to constitute an information explosion in the field. In order to cope with the overload, the Institute of Labor and Industrial Relations of the University of Michigan—Wayne State University in 1966 started *Poverty and Human Resources Abstracts,* a publication which abstracts from various scholarly journals, books, and reports the gist of the great mass of material by the new breed of poverty specialists that appears each month. In setting up this journal, which has a national circulation, the future growth of the field was taken into consideration by wisely including in its contents cross references and key words which will permit computerizing. This implies rightly that the mass of books, articles, and reports on the subject of poverty and related manpower topics is a major effort now, and promises to become even greater.

Dealing with such major topics as poverty, policy, programs, populations, legal assistance, housing, manpower policy, perspectives, and labor mobility, *PHRA* covers in each bimonthly issue about 150 major articles, books, or reports which it abstracts to about 200 words. In addition it gives an index to another 100 to 150 articles. Clearly this plethora of writing is tangible evidence of a high level—in volume at least—of professional activity in poverty.

One category of abstract represented by some 15 to 20 abstracts per month is a summary of the demonstration projects which have been conducted and written up for journals, conference proceedings, colloquia, and seminars. These demonstration projects, and in fact the entire journal, are remarkably silent on the kinds of programs being conducted by private corporations, except for some summary reports produced by the U.S. Chamber of Commerce which are not especially relevant to the mainstream of industry and private sector activity. For the first three issues in 1968, for example, there is nothing which would indicate that the National Alliance for Businessmen even exists, although to the time of publication the Alliance had placed 100,000 ghetto unemployed in jobs. Nor was the name of Henry Ford II, its chairman, whose firm had hired 6,000 ghetto residents during the year, mentioned in the index. This is partially understandable by the very assumptions of the journal. Its policy seems to be that poverty and its cure is a government problem, and that all cures must originate in this quarter. *PHRA* is equally silent on the military programs, and is mainly a report of the writings and speeches of the professional poverty experts. The Upjohn Institute for Unemployment Research, one private sector agency, is, however, well represented and its work fully abstracted.

The Research and Demonstration Program

The ingenuity of the poverty profession is clearly pointed up in the kinds of demonstration grants which it has obtained and executed. Typical of such demonstration grants are the following:

- A study of the nine graduating classes of auto mechanics from two vocational schools. (The whites got better jobs.)

82

- A study of the effects of retraining programs in the San Francisco Bay area.
- A cost benefit study of the effectiveness of MDTA and vocational education in western Massachusetts.
- A study of the effects of a youth-training program for 1,000 youngsters in St. Louis. (Motivation and attitude toward employment affect results achieved.)
- A New York City report on youth training entitled "An Experiment to Test Three Major Issues of Work Program Methodology Within Mobilization for Youth's Integrated Services to Out-of-School Unemployed Youth."
- An evaluation of the Foster Grandparent Program.
- A nine-week work-demonstration program for 170 youths in Pittsburgh.
- The In-School Work-Experience Program in Greater Toledo.
- Evaluation of a neighborhood health project in Washington, D.C.
- An analysis of job satisfaction of employed youth involved in an experimental school drop-out rehabilitation program in Oklahoma.
- Experimental and demonstration manpower project for the recruitment, training, placement, and follow-up of rural unemployed workers in ten north Florida counties.
- "Nineteen Negro Men," a study of a practical nursing program in Detroit.

The list, of course, is typical but not complete, and were it expanded to cover all of the demonstration grants given under Department of Labor, OEO, HEW, and other funding sources, it would be nearly infinite. Are such things, which apparently amuse senators and businessmen, totally without worth, simply because they are esoteric? Clearly not.

83

They demonstrate a concern for people. In many cases a pressing local problem could be solved using government funds only if the persons in charge presented their cause as one appropriate for a "demonstration grant." They got the funds, spent it to get people back to work, or in shape to work, and then in due deference to the sponsor wrote a report with some comments about general application of the idea. No shotgun criticism uttered by a hostile congressman could match the criticism which the experts themselves provide for each other. Daniel Moynihan, Garth Mangum, and Sar Levitan, probably the three leading figures in the new poverty profession, have fired amazingly accurate and painful darts at the efforts to date. Levitan chides his colleagues:

> The academic fraternity has been less than generous in evaluating antipoverty programs. Instead of testing existing present programs, or suggesting alternatives, social scientists are prone to deal with esoteric subjects. Also a lack of operational data about ongoing programs makes the task of evaluation extremely hazardous. A social scientist is more apt to escape behind a mountain of equations rather than deal with real issues. If he is not a numerologist he is more likely to be concerned with the Big Picture, but he still avoids controversial issues.[1]

A 1966 conference at the U.S. Department of Labor dealt with the question of putting research, experimental, and demonstration projects to work. The speakers demonstrated their inability to cope with the transition from a small, pilot framework into a large-scale successful operation which gets at the heart of the problem. Their solutions were almost all in the realm of better management of the demonstration projects being done. Better proposals, better contract negotiations, better interaction between the project people and the sponsors, training the Washington staffs better, and cooperation between the multiple agencies involved in funding demonstration projects seemed to be their answer.

The worst limitations of the demonstration programs have by and large been overlooked. They all avoid the guts of the problem; *every one of them would cost billions if it were to be expanded into a full-dress solution and action program.* Mayor John Lindsay of New York estimates that $50 billion would be the minimum required to make New York a livable city. The cost of making it a decent city, or a good city, would be incalculable. Others have suggested from $150 to $200 billion as the cost of restoring our cities. Garth Mangum points out that really to exploit the advantages of MDTA would take $3 billion a year. Why, then, isn't the money spent?

Because legislators know very well that the tax toleration of their constituency is such that the people will never stand still for the tax bills which would result from trying to fund answers from Washington.

Meanwhile the demonstration grants flow on, in the hope that somehow they can produce in microcosm a method of solving the problem which, when expanded, will somehow produce such attractive results that taxpayers will shell out the money. Congress meanwhile is willing to fund numerous small programs which affect only fragments of the problem, as long as the total cost doesn't run into the politically explosive upper-tax toleration of the voting public. The result is continued frustration and a fairly high level of expenditure without attacking root causes.

The Office of Economic Opportunity tacitly recognized these limitations of federal funding by its organization into Community Action Programs. The attempt here was to prime the pump, to get local groups involved in the programs initially funded from Washington. Frances Piven refers to this as a "federal strategy for local change." This means that the federal government funds local commissions, research studies, projects, and reports as a means of warming up agitation in the local poor community, which in turn will produce hot local action previously cooled by local inertia or interests. Strategies like the demonstration project become instruments of political agitation in the cities, which in turn calls for more federal influence in local communities.[2]

This local agitation aspect of demonstration projects has not gone unnoticed by local politicians, and has produced counterpressures upon Congress to seek out answers to such questions as why the Blackstone Rangers and another Chicago gang, the Red Devils, received heavy dosages of federal funds which allegedly went into uses not envisioned by the sponsors. As Piven points out, the rationale behind having representation of the poor in community action programs and demonstration projects is hardly to improve the administrative efficiency with which these activities are conducted. Rather it is seen as a mean of enlarging the skills of the poor so that they may become an effective force in local affairs. The effect produced is not upon the project, but upon the people who become involved.

M. Rein and S. M. Miller see the demonstration project as a strategy of change, and discount largely the possibilities of its being a pilot project which is being tested for possible extension to a broader base. It has some effect in that it obtains funds in small bites that couldn't be obtained in large ones. The main effects, however, they suggest, are the same that Piven proposes. It is a vehicle whereby the federal government can intervene in the status quo of local arrangements by arousing conflict and confrontation between the poor and the local political or economic establishment.[3]

Thus the ultimate cost effectiveness of demonstration projects cannot be measured by the number of unemployed it puts to work, nor by the number of underemployed who are upgraded. The demonstration project has as its purpose the arousal of conflict, and development of local poor leaders in confrontation with the local establishment, with the agitation it produces as a spillover effect. The end consequences of this increased involvement are unknown, even to those who enlarge it, although it is presumed that since it is in the right direction its consequences must be salubrious.

The effectiveness of the demonstration project is deliberately downgraded in order to emphasize the spillover benefit of a more active citizenship on the part of the poor. If such be the objective—and there is much to be said for

87

the active participation of poor citizens in their government at the local level—the demonstration project does not solve the economic problems of the ghetto.

That solution requires jobs for people. It requires the upgrading of the underemployed to open more positions above the starting levels, and the hiring of people previously considered unqualified at the starting levels. This cannot be done by the convoluted schemes of demonstration projects and massive social reform programs administered from a plethora of Washington agencies. *It must be done by the corporation.*

Jobs for 100,000 people at a normal going wage of $6,000 a year per person would add $600 million to the purchasing power of slum dwellers. With a normal multiplier effect this would contribute vastly more than triple that amount appropriated through government channels. Its effect upon the recipients who became wage earners would be even more revolutionary than the effects of the special demonstration grants upon community action confrontation at local levels. The quality of life from the corporation course would be more immediate, more predictable, and more permanent.

The effects of local confrontation in all likelihood will be a further degradation of the city, rather than an improvement, if it is unaccompanied by private sector jobs. Like the military programs, of themselves agitation-producing programs may be productive of vast harm. Coupled with a private program of job creation, they could be highly beneficial.

7

IS BLACK POWER
A SOLUTION?

That such violent warfare may be
unavoidable is not herein denied. But if
there is the slightest chance to avoid it,
the politics of Black Power . . . is seen as
the only viable hope.

> Stokely Carmichael and
> Charles V. Hamilton,
> BLACK POWER

What Is Black Power?

"The only cure for white racism is Black Power," states Roy
Innis, chairman of the Congress of Racial Equality (CORE).
"The average white has no choice but to be a racist in this
system. I therefore cannot wait around for whites to change
the system so that it will meet my needs." Innis defines
Black Power as

> control by blacks of the institutions that give them goods and
> services. . . . Black people must reject segregation and they
> must equally reject integration as an alternative. In a hetero-
> geneous society such as ours, with clearly defined factions,
> black and white, there are three possible forms of organiza-
> tion. Most people think there are two.[1]

Thus Black Power becomes a form of black nationalism, not unlike that of Jewish nationalism. It also poses the natural necessity of a promised land. Innis added that he would favor some section of New York State as a site for the promised land and "certainly hoped they would not be stuck with Mississippi."[2]

The implications of the Black Power drive are less in finding real estate than in finding a means of establishing a racial mood of self-esteem, pride, racial consciousness, and solidarity. Because these attitudes are the opposite of alienation, apathy, submission, and hostility, they could substantially affect the individual and group behavior of the black people. The Kerner Commission, commenting on Black Power and its effects upon young blacks, states:

> These conditions have created a volatile mixture of attitudes which needs only a spark to ignite mass violence. Strident appeals to violence, heard from white racists, were echoed and reinforced last summer in the inflammatory rhetoric of black racists and militants. Throughout the year, extremists crisscrossed the country preaching a doctrine of black power and violence.[3]

The phrase Black Power, first used at the time of James Meredith's march from Memphis to Jackson in 1966, evoked a tremor of fear and dismay when first uttered, and its meaning was not as clearly enunciated as Innis stated it in his Ann Arbor speech in 1968. What does it mean, beyond black identity?

1. *It means independent political power.* In this sense it could be represented by the election of Carl Stokes as

mayor of Cleveland, or Carl Hatcher as mayor of Gary, Ind. It could mean voter registration drives in the Deep South, where the majority of the population is black, and subsequently the election of black sheriffs, legislators, and congressmen from these districts.

2. *In economic terms* it can mean creating separate independent black businesses, not only by loans and consulting advice to blacks who wish to form or expand businesses, but by creation of cooperatives in the South. In education it can mean control of schools in the ghettos by black representation on boards. It also means that the market power of the black people in the slum could be used to influence the business firms which do business there. In some instances Black Power is represented by boycotts of certain businesses which fail to employ blacks. The suggestion of utopian societies, perhaps apart from the rest of society, is a relatively new and not especially well thought-through objective.

3. *Social separatism,* in the sense of isolated states like the socialist communities, or perhaps the cooperative societies of the past century, or perhaps the *kibbutzim* in modern Israel, is something which only a few of the black leaders espouse. Others, such as Roy Wilkins, oppose it. The record of such societies, operating unassisted and disconnected from the larger society, shows little promise. Marcus Garvey in 1914 proposed that the blacks flee their oppressors, since the racism of whites would never be ameliorated. He proposed a wholesale migration of American blacks to Africa, and insisted that the black develop a distinct racial type of society of his own by a return to

91

the motherland. At the same time Garvey was organizer of a number of businesses including hotels, restaurants, a printing plant, and a steamship line. He was ultimately deported for having used the mails to defraud.

The possibility of an *apartheid* such as exists in South Africa would of course be an immediate trigger for open revolution. Black laborers in the mines and industries of this white-dominated nation, who comprise over three-fourths of the population, live in separate communities to which they must return after work, and exist under a tight system of passes, scrutiny, and undercover operatives who quickly snuff out any attempts to break the color bar.

Another group favoring a separate black nation are the Black Muslims. They seek a part of America's land for a separate nation away from the "white devils." Cassius Clay, or Muhammed Ali, is one noted figure in the movement. Another was Malcolm X, whose original last name was Little, but who dropped the name because of its origin from a slave-owning family in his past. Malcolm X quit the Muslims in 1964 to establish his own Organization of Afro-American Unity. In 1965 he was shot and killed at a rally of his organization in New York City. Two Muslims were among those arrested.

4. *Militarism as Black Power.* Still another version of Black Power is one which has been espoused by the young black militants. At a Black Power conference in Newark, N.J., in July of 1967, a series of militant resolutions was enacted. One of these called for the division of the country into black and white nations. Christianity was labeled "a white religion" and it was added that "every black church

and all religious institutions that do not join the black revolution shall be boycotted, ostracized, criticized, publicized, and rejected by the black community." Other resolutions at Newark called for:

- Black-controlled financial institutions supported by bonds to establish neighborhood credit unions and housing and building loans.
- Paramilitary training for all black youth.
- A national holiday to honor black heroes.
- A black university with subsidiary units in many cities.
- A school to train black political organizers.
- A buy-black movement to bring economic pressure to bear on employers to employ more blacks.

The Newark meeting was attended by representatives of 45 activist groups.

The Corporation and Black Power

Given four different interpretations of Black Power, what are the interests of the corporation in Black Power? Briefly they can be summarized as follows:

1. The corporation has a strong interest in avoiding violence and militancy which could lead to insurrection, guerrilla warfare, and anarchy.

93

2. The corporation can afford to be neutral to political implications, but should favor a general tendency toward strong citizen participation in politics. This participation will undoubtedly cause a rising level of demand for government services and rising costs of government, but that outcome is vastly preferable to such services being withheld and riots generating as a result.

3. The corporation can afford to be neutral to the question of whether blacks are integrated into white communities and the white middle class or whether they prefer to remain in segregated all-black areas, enjoying the benefits of prosperity and civil liberties within a culture of their own.

4. The corporation must assume active leadership in providing economic strength and viability to blacks everywhere. Primarily this will mean jobs, but it could also mean job creation through financing, supporting, and establishing businesses in primarily black areas. This requires that companies which previously had fled the cities with their new plants and offices reverse the movement and build in the city. The infusion of private funds, especially from the large insurance companies into urban housing investment, is another. Job creation through establishment of businesses in the ghetto areas alone isn't the answer; there are already businesses in these places. The problem is that businesses in these inner cities are often run by a person whose low standards of business practice would be unthinkable in a corporation with a socially attuned management and an eye to public relations. The merchant who raises his prices on the day welfare checks are issued, the

sandbagger who gulls innocent people into his store with grandiose signs announcing bargains, which prove to be somewhat different when the customer enters, are part of the apparatus which exploits the black and produces resentment. Chicago slumlords charge an average of $20 more per month to blacks than to whites. The federal government's Small Business Administration between 1954 and 1964 made only seven loans to black businessmen.

> **A significant need exists to improve the quality of business practices and business management for private enterprise conducted in the inner city. The corporation most certainly has the strength and the know-how to achieve this upgrading.**

At present the slum merchant represents the free enterprise system to the black community. As Stokely Carmichael sees it, the white middle-class business community looks like this:

> Many of its members sneak into the black community by day, exploit it, and take the money home to their middle-class communities to support their operas and art galleries and comfortable homes. When not actually robbing they will fight off the handful of more affluent black people who seek to move in.[4]

The essence of Black Power does not lie in violence, nor in jobs. It lies in the self-definition of the black race. The process may of course include terrorism and guerrilla action if need be, but they are possible, not necessary, elements. Political growth and sophistication are one part of the necessary pattern. Economic growth and improvement of the quality of life, whether in integrated suburbs or racially integrated but satisfactory urban life, is another. It demands decent housing, jobs, and markets which permit the inhabitants of whatever race to share in the fruits of a healthy free enterprise system.

It can hardly be expected that the black will be a staunch advocate of a superior economic system unless he shares in its benefits. If he does participate in it fully, it is hard to imagine that he will become a force which would disrupt and overthrow it.

Moving plants back into the inner city is a possible corporate action that will have many advantages for the residents. Jobs will be within easy reach. A two-hour bus ride with three transfers to get to a factory reduces the likelihood of blacks seeking and keeping a position there. A labor market which is within realistic travel distance from the inner city means that the inner city dwellers will be employed, and their income will be spent there. It also adds to the tax base, which supports public services in the inner city, including schools. IBM's announcement of a new plant to be built in the Bedford-Stuyvesant section of Brooklyn, Control Data's new component plant in a poor Minneapolis area, and Avco's printing plant in the Roxbury section of Boston are illustrative of this trend. Admittedly this will add to the cost of operation at first glance. Yet, by drawing on the good will generated by this move, an innovative management might well find that it is able to generate higher levels of cooperation and individual productivity than is possible in many conventionally located plants.

New Business Creation

The creation of new business, led and staffed by black management, is a possibility which also shows some potential. Here lies an opportunity for larger firms to employ less skilled people without being handicapped by the combination of high wage levels and elaborate work rules which often characterize unionized plants. It will also avoid the problems of an established business in which technical specialties comprise a basis for the major product.

One example of such a creation is Barfield Cleaners of Ypsilanti, Mich. Johnny Barfield, a black small businessman, owns and operates a building-cleaning service. A large aerospace research company nearby engaged him to take over all cleaning functions on a contract basis. Not stopping here, the management of the larger corporation provided some expert managerial advice to Barfield in hiring and training employees. Filmstrip training guides were made; organization planning and modern marketing knowhow were provided. As a result, Barfield Cleaners has become a substantial small business, employing the best techniques of modern management. The larger firm gets excellent service, at costs which are competitive with hiring people at its customary high rates. Barfield pays above-average rates to employees for cleaning and janitorial work, and has created many supervisory and clerical positions, thus disproving the claim that janitorial work is a "dead end" occupation.

Business cooperation of this kind in creating and upgrading such service occupations as guarding, janitorial service, and maintenance can best bring modern managerial skills to bear, and perhaps avert the greatest danger in this approach: that these businesses might fail due to the managerial incompetence of the new black entrepreneur. This of course doesn't imply that the black businessman has any natural monopoly on bad management. The rate of business failures in this country is such that small businesses are more apt to fail than succeed. The reason, Dun and Bradstreet reports, is bad management.

Simply establishing small businesses in the slums, only to leave them in the hands of untrained managers, ultimately to fail, will hardly alleviate the situation. Even with trained managers they may fail, but the deliberate, systematic infusion of managerial skills through assignment to training experts and advisers can keep such failures to a minimum.

The idea has numerous possibilities in retailing, gasoline distribution, wholesaling, and service occupations. Creating the concept of career planning and development and self-development as enterprising men, while somewhat removed from the popular image of Black Power, would certainly meet all of its requirements, even those of Stokely Carmichael. The consequences would be highly beneficial to the corporation which underwrote it, supported it, and employed its services.

98

THE NEGRO MARKET– A POSITIVE REASON FOR BUSINESS ACTION

Of all of the intellectual achievements of
Western Civilization, the one I think that
is most truly civilized is that by and large
we have learned to deal with man as he is
or, at most, as he seems capable of
becoming but not as we suppose in the
abstract that he ought to be. Our
economy is geared to human acquisitive-
ness and our politics to human ambition.
                    Sen. J. William Fulbright,
                    THE ARROGANCE OF POWER

Black people today represent a market segment that
spends $30 billion and includes 23 million consumers. The
population and buying power of the blacks is rising. By
providing them with jobs, the corporation adds to that buying power. The rise in black population from 1960 to 1966
was 14.2 percent, an increase which compares with a
growth of 8.6 percent in the white population for the same
period of time. By 1970 one out of seven Americans will be
black, and corresponding increases are predicted for the
future. Seventy percent of the black population lives in the

99

major marketing areas of the United States. Table 7 shows some of the projections of black population in urban areas in the years ahead.

Table 7

The Negro Population in the Central City

(percentage of Total City Population)

| DATE | PRESUMING THAT | |
	WHITE POPULATION (CITY) REMAINS CONSTANT	WHITE POPULATION IN CITIES DECLINES AS RATE BLACK GAINS
1966 (actual)	20.6%	20.6%
1975	25.6%	27.3%
1985	31.0%	35.6%

Source: Kerner Commission Report; U.S. Bureau of the Census.

If the future growth of cities resembles the past, it is entirely possible that 35 percent of the population of the cities will be black by 1985. The income of blacks is equal to about 55 percent of that of whites. While the income and purchasing power of both groups is increasing, there are some distinct economic advantages in looking at the black market. Its importance is illustrated by the percentage of customers it comprises in at least two major urban centers, Detroit and Chicago. According to *Men's Wear* magazine, 45 percent of Detroit's J. L. Hudson customers in the downtown store are black, as are 25 percent of Marshall Field's customers.

The size of the black market could be substantially increased in the future, not only in numbers, which appears inevitable, but in incomes, if unemployment and poverty were eliminated through a comprehensive job program. For example, if the differential between white and black per capita income were cut in half, the added market would come to about $7 billion. If the gap between the two races' incomes were closed by 1985, the added purchasing power would range from a probable $45 billion to a possible high of $52 billion annually. This last sum is greater than the gross national product prior to World War II for the entire nation, white and black. To look backward, the market loss between 1960 and 1966 which might have been realized if the blacks had been fully employed is, by my estimate, $61 billion (based on data from *Marketing Insights* and Bureau of Census figures). This immense loss of market should be of concern to corporations whose lifeblood lies in getting a share of the market, and even more importantly, causing the total market size to expand.

What we are talking about is essentially a basic feature of capitalism. As Joseph Schumpeter put it:

> The capitalist engine is first and last an engine of mass production which unavoidably means also production for the masses, whereas, climbing upward in the scale of individual incomes, we find that the increasing proportion is being spent on personal services and on handmade commodities, the prices of which are largely a function of wage rates. . . . Queen Elizabeth owned silk stockings. The capitalist achievement does not typically consist of providing more silk stockings for queens but in bringing them within reach of working girls in return for steadily decreasing amounts of effort.[1]

The basic point here isn't an especially esoteric one. The economic rise of the black man comprises a kind of economic revolution, certainly equal to the space program,

101

foreign aid, and even a minor war in its beneficial economic effects if we are smart enough to see the fact and capitalize on it. The real question is how, as hard-nosed businessmen, we could have been so oblivious for so long as not to have noted the economic potential here. The Conference of Southern Governors in 1951 finally abandoned the drive to snare cheap little firms to go South and pay subsistence wages. They resolved that their purpose in the future would be to bring in the high-wage industries: the General Electrics, the Boeings, and the Lockheeds, who would pay high wages which in turn would be spent, thus creating demand for capital goods, which in turn would be a generator of demand for consumer goods.

The lead time left to save the private enterprise system is shorter than it might be. The corporation has systematically aimed its marketing programs at the middle-class market, in which there are some blacks. In doing so, however, it has also restricted its employment policies to prevent substantial segments of the population from joining that economic middle class. The resulting poverty and its consequences open the distinct possibility that governmental controls and special subsidies will expand greatly to increase and stabilize employment, and these measures will comprise a direct attack upon the essential ability of corporations to maneuver freely in the marketplace.

Few think in terms of the vast productive and distribution capacity of the private enterprise system as the solution to the urban problem. In part this is because the corporations themselves have assumed little leadership in behaving as if they had solutions.

The Buying Behavior of Blacks

Conventional marketing techniques may not suffice of themselves if this high potential market is to be tapped. The most important fact for the corporation to bear in mind is one which requires setting aside the single-minded application of the "marketing concept." It is briefly this:

The black market is one which must be created and sold by the corporation, both being done at the same time.

The assumption which often lies behind the marketing concept is that "everything starts when the sale is made." This is a situational and rather special application of capitalism. Given a middle-class society in which everyone—or almost everyone—is employed, such as we have pictured to date, the major problem is selling, advertising, and merchandising. While the end purpose and overriding objective of capitalism is consumption, it will become apparent in the future in the black market that *black employment and black consumption must go on concurrently,* or the whole process grinds to a halt. Selling consumer durables to residents of an underdeveloped country is more than creating a desire to buy. It requires simultaneously the creation of the wherewithal to express these desires in the market.

The second important fact about the buying behavior of blacks is that income which could be applied to the purchase of goods may not be spent according to practices in the general market. Norman Skinner, Director of the National Negro Marketing Institute, has noted that the top-selling brands in the white market are not the top-selling brands in the black market, and adds, "If you don't know anything about us, you can't sell us."[2]

Black Power in the Market

The willingness of the black to boycott people who are not respectful of him as a person, or of blacks as a race, is readily apparent. A Philadelphia petroleum company learned this to its dismay in the fifties, and numerous communities in all parts of the North and South have found this an effective tool for bringing merchants into line. The consumer vote is a potent instrument as the size of the black market increases. A number of persons have noted that the rising pride of blacks in their race, the rising realization that blacks do not want to be white, will affect their behavior, including buying behavior.

The most obvious casualty of the rising militancy of blacks in the sixties has been the fiction that the typical black man is an ambling, amiable, and somehow humorous nitwit. This is the first factor in assessing the black market. The black man is perfectly able to distinguish his friends from his foes, and he will do so readily in expressing his rising market power. What kinds of programs are most likely to achieve a solid position in the black market?

1. *The total company approach.* The firm which employs no blacks on its sales force, in its service organization, in

104

its factories, and in its staff and managerial positions may ultimately lose out to those companies that do. The communication systems between blacks is improving steadily, and the ever present possibility of boycotts, total or partial, can have an effect upon ability to capture a market.

2. *Personal selling revisited.* The retailer especially will find that some retraining of his sales persons to cope with the rising numbers of black consumers may be in order. In many ways the same things that cause white customers to return again and again will bring black customers back to buy. Product knowledge, courtesy, friendliness, and respectful treatment are always desirable features in selling. The antiwhite bias of blacks is not a chronic problem. As one study has shown, the attitude of blacks to whites is a function of the white attitudes toward them. A general tendency to await initiating action by the white is a commonly observed reaction. Equal treatment is a key ingredient.[3]

An assumption that blacks are interested only in the bargain basement can be degrading and lose business if the assumption is false. Denial to blacks of service given to everyone else is quickly spotted, and they go elsewhere. The visible presence of some black clerks and sales support people is an asset in selling to a predominantly black clientele. Tokenism is usually recognized, but is considered by the black consumer to be better than nothing. It may not be enough in the future.

3. *Reaching the consumer with information.* TV commercials aimed at the general market may or may not persuade black people. Radio, according to *Sponsor* magazine, is a more widely used medium, and black media seem to have

a greater effect than ordinary media in reaching black consumers. The effectiveness of commercials is often a function of the personalities delivering them, and those delivered by blacks are by and large more effective than commercials to whites over white media. The ability of the listener to identify with the person delivering the message has an important effect. The credibility of the black disc jockey has been found to be high among black buyers, higher for example than that of a smoothly professional white announcer delivering a white-centered commercial.

A number of important newspapers, the *Afro-American* in Baltimore, the Pittsburgh *Courier, Ebony,* and *Jet* are among the best examples of media that reach black markets and affect buying behavior.

4. *Product and service mix.* The consumption patterns of blacks have emerged from a century of a special pattern of life, and do not resemble white habits closely. As one operator of a black radio station put it: "He is anxous to possess items which serve as status symbols of achievement and equality and will buy premium items as he is able to afford them."[4] Consumer durables such as cars, TV sets, radios, electric mixers, and refrigerators are apt to be among the first preferences of blacks as their income rises. In other items, preferences are apt to run to the highest quality levels which can be afforded; for example, 50 percent of the Scotch whisky purchased in the United States is bought by blacks. National brands have a preferential position over private brands, if there is no reason for the black man to believe that its producer has a bad record in hiring blacks; if it does, he'll simply turn to another well-known

106

brand which has no such odious reputation in this respect.

5. *Price and nonprice buying behavior.* Not long ago a large credit company, a division of an automobile company, decided to do its bit and open an office in a slum to make available to black people credit for consumer durables. While the company's business acumen was not doubted in most ways, it made a major error when it decided to make the interest rates for this office higher than that of all its other offices. Shortly after the office started business, the national headquarters was visited by a pair of soft-spoken black businessmen. In a quiet way they informed the general manager of the division that what the firm was doing was gouging. They alluded to what might happen to the new office should disorders occur in that section of the city. They also implied that certain organizations would boycott that company's product if the company insisted upon the higher rate, including the add-ons. After a reasonable discussion, the company agreed to reduce the rate. The two black callers agreeably proposed that if the company could show after six months of operation that losses were excessively high, then they would be happy to discuss the company's results and possibly cooperate with a sufficient increase to cover actual losses.

Such conversations are apt to become increasingly prevalent as corporations enter the black market in the future. The black market is anomalous in some respects. (1) The Negro buyer is not especially price-sensitive in terms of quality. He will generally buy a higher-priced prestige item over a less expensive but less prestigeful product. (2) He is extremely price-sensitive if he sees any evidence of discriminatory pricing which raises prices for black outlets.

As a merchandising manager for J. L. Hudson, the giant Detroit department store, put it:

> I think the reason we have such a clutch on the Negro buyer is in our twofold policy of selling prestige and high-quality goods, coupled with the fact that we state that our policy is, "We will not be undersold." The Negro woman is a pretty skilled comparison shopper, not so much for low price, but for evidence of discriminatory pricing.

A key point in understanding black-buyer behavior is the presence of militants, who will serve a more active function in moving against manufacturers and retailers who appear to engage in discriminatory business practice. Under the milder form of this pressure, the manufacturer will find that he loses market. Under its more active form, the retailer may discover himself standing on a pile of smoking rubble.

The Economic Effects of Full Employment

Unemployment and underemployment of any significant segment of the population comprise a weakness in the economy. The requirements of economic growth are such that workers who produce are able to consume their own production at a rate which allows a certain amount of their income to be channeled into savings and into investment.

Underemployed people, those at the lower end of the income scale, will consume all they earn. As their income rises, their consumption will rise, but not proportionately. This means that in a high-wage economy more money will be available for savings in one form or another: equity in a house, insurance, retirement plans, and the like. This money is then available for investment through private investors. This private investment will be channeled into capital enlargement, which increases the productivity of the worker, making it possible for his income to be enlarged through higher wages.

Consumption and investment work in an arrangement known to the economist as an accelerator system. The enlargement of consumption creates a demand for goods, which in turn creates a demand for further capital goods, machines, plants, transportation equipment, etc. This demand further creates jobs for people making these capital items and servicing them. These capital goods workers become consumers, and thus the added investment into new capital goods works with what is called the multiplier effect on consumption.

More than a simple theory, the system works in practice. Take the case of Sam X, who lives in a black area just off Grand Boulevard in Detroit. After dropping out of school in 1961, Sam sought a job but was unable to find steady work. He washed cars, handed out leaflets, and did some other casual laborer jobs. One summer he went to Traverse City to pick cherries with a job promised, but had trouble with the picking machine, since he got there a day late and didn't have time to learn to operate the picker. After three

109

days he was demoted and given a casual labor job. In a week he returned to Detroit. That fall he was picked up with three others in a getaway car fleeing from a liquor store robbery. He was sentenced to a boy's correction farm, where he stayed for two years and was then paroled. Upon discharge he hung around the corner, did occasional jobs, and ran numbers until he was picked up for parole violation and sent to the House of Correction for three months. Upon discharge he arranged a common law marriage and became the father of two children. When the Aid to Dependent Children for Unemployed came around he disappeared. He moved two miles away, and left his family better off under ADC than if he were living with them.

In 1967 a recruiter for Ford Motor Company talked to a minister in a church where Sam had been receiving handouts from time to time. Sam reported to a Ford office in the slum area and was interviewed. He expected that when they heard of his record he would be rejected, but he was told, "If you agree to show up for work every day, we have a job for you." An arrangement was made for him to ride with another Ford employee to the engine plant at the River Rouge branch of Ford Motor Company. He paid the driver two dollars a week for his share of the gas. The first day on the job, his supervisor, who was black, emphasized again the importance of coming in every day. A week later he went to a party over the weekend and on Monday took the day off. He received a telephone call that day from his foreman. That night two of his fellow workers, one a shop steward in the United Automobile Workers, visited him and asked him where he had been.

"I took the day off, I wasn't feeling well. What difference does it make? The company didn't have to pay me, so they didn't lose anything."

The next day he went to work and the foreman explained that showing up every day was important. The idea that Ford *needed him* and that Ford didn't save any money if he didn't come in was impressed upon him. After that he showed up regularly. His hourly pay was $3.45 an hour straight time. After a month he worked Saturdays, for which he was paid $41.40 for the day, almost the equivalent of a week's pay at washing cars.

On the sixth week he returned to his family. His common law wife had been working and continued to do so part-time. They purchased some new furniture, an iron, and a color TV set. On Saturday night they went to a local tavern and ate dinner, watched the show, talked with friends, and drank. The kids got new clothes and some toys. For the next six months they spent steadily on clothes and more appliances; they bought a new middle-priced car on credit, and a roomful of new furniture, also on credit.

Sam's earnings for the first year were reduced by a month-long strike, during which time he served on the picket line and received partial pay for that. When he wasn't picketing he washed cars to keep up the payments. When he returned to work the department went on ten hours, six days a week. As a result, during his first year he earned $8,390. His major complaint was the amount of income tax withheld. A union official told him he should declare his common law wife as a dependent, which he did.

In the spring of 1968 he and his wife decided to start

saving money for a down payment on their own home. He was advised by his foreman that the credit union would pay good interest on deposits and would help him when he was ready to take out a loan. The credit union official went over his budget with him, and worked out a savings plan. Sam states that, under some pressure from his wife, he is considering marriage after he buys the house.

The unusual feature of this story is that five years ago it might never have happened. Sam might possibly have been hired, even with his record, at Ford, but he had no practical way of knowing where and how to apply, or that he would be accepted if he did so.

As a result of the fact that Ford's policy changed to compel recruiters to go into the slums to seek out unemployed, Sam is now an economic contributor. Sam's story has been multiplied 6,000 times at Ford since the riots of 1967 in Detroit, and 30,000 times in all of Detroit at Chrysler, General Motors, Michigan Bell, Detroit Edison, and numerous other firms. In conservative terms, about $180 million in added income was infused into Detroit. After taking away taxes, the consumption portion of this figure would run about $90 to $100 million. Its accelerator effect would be more difficult to estimate.

There's small doubt, however, that it has been extremely good business to hire Sam and the 30,000 like him. Even if Sam should later take part in a riot (most rioters were employed), the net gain would be high.

The gains to Sam's family, to society, and to reduced cost of government, and numerous other benefits, are a spillover.

9

ACTION AT THE TOP

If we businessmen aren't going to take a
major role in tackling and eventually
solving the problems in our cities, then
who will?

Gerard Philippe,
Chairman, General Electric Company,
THE NEGRO AND THE CITY

Corporate leaders are already deeply involved in hiring the disadvantaged. The extent of this corporate commitment to the solution of a pressing social problem is on a scale which matches its production effort in World War II and the Korean War. The results to date have been heartening and instructive to those who have dragged their feet. The major outcome?

- Hard experience has demonstrated that persons previously considered unemployable can be *hired* and then *made qualified,* and in fact become productive employees.
- Early successes have encouraged many of the more reluctant to step up to the task, and a general climate of cooperation and action prevails, especially among top management.

113

Top Management Moves

The New Detroit Committee, formed after the riots of 1967, is without doubt one of the most high powered of any of the local or regional groups organized to cope with the urban crisis. Headed by J. L. Hudson, Jr., chief of the J. L. Hudson department store, the city's largest, it numbers in its ranks James Roche, Chairman of General Motors, the world's largest corporation; Henry Ford II, chairman of the third largest corporation; and Lynn Townsend, chairman of Chrysler, the fifth largest corporation. Others of equal standing in their own firms have actively worked at devising programs in the area of jobs, housing, and community development for the slum dwellers. As a direct result of the work of the NDC 12,000 workers were hired in the member firms alone. Even more were taken on in other firms who cooperated with their effort.

The beginning at Ford Motor Company was not in 1967, but many years before. As with General Motors and Chrysler, it had been Ford's common practice to hire drop-outs and selected ex-convicts, and under the earlier government-sponsored Plans for Progress campaigns, voluntary programs had been vigorously executed. Yet, prior to the 1967 riots, the remnants of "testing as usual" had been applied in order to keep the qualification level of workers high.

The significance of the 1967 riots lies in their effect upon selection standards. As Mr. Phillippe stated recently:

Businessmen are looking with increased interest at their own standards of job qualification and disqualification to see if they

114

cannot, by changing some of them, make it easier to accommodate disadvantaged people. For example, I think we must break down the credential barriers that have long existed in industry.

One of the more significant documents produced in the modern corporation in recent years is the famous "Blue Letter" issued by Henry Ford II, chairman of Ford Motor Company (see Appendix). It is apparent that here is a full commitment to hiring persons who were previously considered unemployable.

Personal commitment of the very top managers of major corporations to making these programs work is an essential first step. Although there are many problems of execution, it is certain that, with the persistent direction of the top policy makers, the problems will be solved. The extent of the personal knowledge of chief executives where these programs now exist is evidenced by their knowledge of details which would not ordinarily occupy the attention of the top people, unless the program involved were considered of major importance to the basic objectives of the firm.

Chrysler's president, Virgil Boyd, for example, explained many of the detailed problems which his company faced in placing 750 hard-core unemployed. These problems included buying glasses for an employee so that he could learn enough reading for simple jobs, or teaching another how to catch a bus in the morning. Employees who signed an X for their pay had to be trained to read "in" and "out" signs on the doors, or had to be taught to count in order to know how many boxes to pile on a truck. They needed to be supplied with an alarm clock in order to get up to get to work.

Raytheon's Chairman, Charles Adams, reported on one group of trainees hired by his firm. "We pick them up by chartered bus at 7:15 each morning, in the heart of the Roxbury section." After a day at training they are bussed home at night. They are paid $1.75 while training, and hired by Raytheon if they complete the training.

Arthur Banes, Vice President of Polaroid, reports that his firm established a plant in the ghetto, and further arranges transfers to suburban plants for those who succeed in this inner city plant. Its main product is a flow of employees, moving on to permanent career job opportunities in other companies (and also Polaroid), especially outside the inner city community.

William Zisch, Vice Chairman of Aerojet General, describes the operation of Watts Manufacturing Company, which was established under a black president in the Los Angeles black community. After an investment of $1.3 million, the company obtained a contract for hospital tents for the military service. It is presently expanding into metal products and wood products. Over 5,000 applied for the first 500 jobs. Problems included high turnover and absenteeism. "We hired people without restrictions. We didn't care if they had police records or whether they had ever held a job before. All we expected was a willingness to work and ability to respond to minimal training."

Lockheed Aircraft has an experimental program for hiring blacks and other minorities, and training them to be qualified. In their Sunnyvale, Calif. plant and Marietta, Ga.

116

plant several hundred hard-core unemployed have been taken in. A majority are minority group members, and a significant number have police records. Yet the program is working.

The National Alliance of Businessmen

While some companies have initiated actions and executed them on their own, others have found that cooperation with existing governmental programs has been worthwhile. Under the Manpower Development and Retraining Act a number of in-plant courses were conducted, leading to employment of graduates.

The major program entailing joint cooperation between government and industry with impact on hiring blacks has been the Concentrated Employment Program (CEP). Launched in January 1968, it was given a new life in President Johnson's manpower report and has worked with considerable success. This success in finding jobs may be attributed in large part to a group headed by the National Alliance of Businessmen (NAB) which pledged the finding of 100,000 new jobs for disadvantaged people by summer 1968 and 500,000 by 1971. It also pledged to try the placement of 200,000 summer positions for youngsters, and in this latter program has fallen short. The adult program has been more than successful, with over 110,000 new jobs pledged by midyear of 1968.[1]

117

The cooperative nature of the program included requests by government that the NAB members seek out such job vacancies, and the response in the form of executive and staff time to solicit firms for their cooperation was great. The government also appropriated $55 million for the program, most of which would be administered by the Labor Department.

The unemployed persons affected are mainly the very hard core. They are illiterate, or have other serious shortcomings which make it highly unlikely that they will succeed even if hired for the most simple work. Under the CEP program, which operated under the acronym of JOBS (Job Opportunity in the Business Sector), the employer hired the marginal worker, and put him immediately into training in such things as reading simple signs, and other rudimentary abilities such as those described above by Mr. Boyd. During this training period they are paid about $1.75 per hour, which is reimbursable by a grant from the government. Each trainee continues his basic educational program until he is ready for trial at a factory position such as press operator, stock handler, assembler, and in some cases welder and metal finisher. Once in this position he is paid the going union rate for the position, which in the automobile industry in 1968 was $3.45 an hour. Because his skills are normally somewhat less than those of better-educated or otherwise more advanced persons, he is hardly worth that rate. The government continues to pay a subsidy for the difference between what the man is actually worth as an employee and the pay he receives. This is in the form of a grant to the company.

Ford, in July 1967, received a $1.7 million grant to give 250 critically hard-core unemployed training under this program.[2] Chrysler was already deeply involved in a similar program for 700 of the hard core. In some instances the actual training of the hard core has been subcontracted to nonprofit organizations who teach the trainees reading and other social and attitude-building skills. These subcontracts often comprise the major cost of the program, for once the new employees enter the plant they normally come up to expected production standards fairly soon after arriving on the job.

The assumptions behind such programs are revolutionary in modern industry. Literacy is seen as an employment requirement only if literacy is a requirement for job success. If an X on the payroll voucher is the only requirement, then training could very plausibly stop there, although such cases would be rare. The worker, for example, must be able to read the names of the buses and their destinations, or he might never get to work. Unable to read warning signs, he might wander into hazardous areas.

Many have suggested that such subsidy of the marginal worker could be an effective alternative to the negative income tax.

1. The system pays the worker the going rates in the labor market for actually working to the best of his abilities, whatever they may be. Thus, he finds an unfavorable consequence for not working and a favorable consequence for working. Some feel that the negative income tax would present favorable consequences for not working and only marginal rewards for the added effort of working. The nor-

mal attitude of the hard core would thus become "Why work?"

2. The company obtains value for value in the employment relationship. It pays the worker for his actual contribution, and pays him the full rate. The difference between the true contribution and the actual pay check is subsidized by governmental grant.

One limitation here is in the nature of work in many technologically advanced businesses. If the man isn't worth the going rate on some jobs he is, in fact, worthless to the firm. The worker on the assembly line who lacks the physical capacity or mental and manual dexterity to keep up with the line may prove very costly. Putting a steering wheel on every third car costs more than the difference in hourly rate between the man who can only operate at this one-third-level effort and the man who can provide a steering wheel for every car presented to him for such service. In technically based businesses such as chemicals and pharmaceuticals, where the product requires great purity, or is for human consumption, error-free effort is part of the product, and the savings are not merely in effort expended but in problem-solving ability and speed of response to signals from the production system.

Despite these limitations, the general concept has sufficiently wide application that undoubtedly it will find a welcoming response. As at least a partial alternative to the negative income tax, it may alleviate some of the cost of $8 billion which some calculate the NIT would involve. Since the negative income tax would still be viable for the aged, mothers with small children who cannot work, and the physically handicapped who cannot work, the costs would still be substantial. Cooperative programs between industry and government of the JOBS type may be expected to be expanded in the future.

The Key Corporate Policy Issues

A recent issue of *Industrial Relations News* reported that many personnel men are now for the first time getting backing for the kind of constructive human relations programs that heretofore they had been bootlegging and smuggling into their practices without top management endorsement. It is obvious that the issue is no longer one of some staff department's having a pet rabbit which it is cultivating to become a corporate tiger. The key first step is how to get a clear company policy statement from the very highest levels of the corporation.

Unless the policy of hiring unemployables starts with the board of directors, or at least with the chief executive, the corporate response will be inadequate.

In the definition of corporate policy on employing the disadvantaged, a range of possible policy statements could

121

be envisioned. The first of these is spelled out in Figure 3.

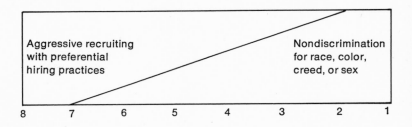

FIGURE 3.
Range of possible policy statements on employment of disadvantaged.

Those firms which state their policy as being between 1 and 2 in Figure 3 are merely obeying the law. There is no special distinction in this, except that such a policy, firmly applied, just skirts being in the dubious company of a lamentably large number of firms who do not adhere to even this minimum standard, and fight the issues through evasions.

A policy which declares nondiscrimination for race, color, creed, or sex, while it adheres to Title VII of the federal law, is in fact discriminatory.

Professor Marshall makes this clear in a statement showing the factors responsible for racial employment patterns.[3] The ostensible policies have nothing to do with racial discrimination, but their specific and immediate effect is the same as if they were racially discriminatory, and *the archi-tects of such policies fully realize this effect.* The nonracial factors that Marshall points out which are knowingly used to bring about discrimination are these:

1. Easy identification with inferior status causes blacks to seek out the stereotyped positions for which blacks are ordinarily employed, such as porter, laborer, and the like.

2. Knowledge of available jobs is limited by segregated places of residence, and low degree of association with people who work in such occupations.

3. Education is shorter for blacks than for whites, since the blacks believe, fairly accurately, that education won't produce economic improvement. The average black college graduate will earn less than the average white high school graduate.

4. Selection systems which are based upon educational background, requiring grammar school for employment, high school for office work, and college degrees for managerial positions, have become a managerial substitute for more reasonable and realistic standards of selection.

5. Vocational training for blacks either doesn't exist or is inadequate, except in certain of the black colleges. The result is a skill barrier which unions and management use to block apprenticeships to black youths. This skill barrier is pictured as imposing a ceiling upon progress, and it in fact results in the young black man not being hired at all, lest he should acquire enough seniority to demand a trial in the apprentice program.

At the other extreme of Figure 3 is a policy of aggressive

123

recruiting with preferential hiring practices which stay within the law, but in practice comprise a *de facto* preferential treatment of blacks. Running a bus from the ghetto to the plant will in all likelihood effectuate the hiring of a larger number of blacks. A recruiter who enters a pool hall or a black church, or who recruits on a street corner in Harlem, may be objectively unbiased and not discriminate. In other words he may state with complete integrity that he will hire every likely applicant who happens to be in the black pool hall, without regard to race, creed, or color. This is legal.

Points 2 to 7 on the scale in Figure 3 represent intermediate positions between these two extreme positions. To start, it might be interesting to ask the typical board of directors to check off on this scale where they picture their company's practices at the present time and where they would like to see them at specific times in the future.

Personnel Vice President Bill Machaver of Sun Chemical has suggested that any policy more than five years old should be reviewed, and if necessary, changed. Such might well be a sensible approach here.

(1.) The farther a company has been to the right, the more it might move toward a timely but possibly temporary position on the left.

(2.) When a balanced position has been achieved it is possible that a company might amend its policy. The most important thing is that top management should *know where it stands at present* and make a positive policy decision for the next year or two years which will help alleviate any results of past imbalances.

124

Should a Company Use Governmental Aid?

Another policy matter which should be decided by the board or the senior officers is to what extent to use governmental assistance in making the hiring of the disadvantaged work. Figure 4 shows a possible range of positions on this question:

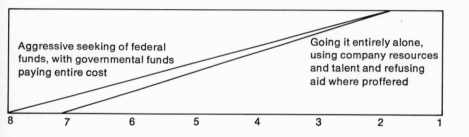

Aggressive seeking of federal funds, with governmental funds paying entire cost

Going it entirely alone, using company resources and talent and refusing aid where proffered

8   7   6   5   4   3   2   1

FIGURE 4.
Range of possible policy positions with respect to using federal subsidies to support special effort in employment.

Going it alone without any government assistance has much to commend it for the large corporation. The reasons, experience has shown, are reasonably persuasive:

1. The paper work entailed in government aid often eats up any economic gains, occupies the time of high-paid people, and adds immensely to the simple work load and the confusion involved. Government aid stipulates certain procedures, some of which have more to do with auditing procedure than with people or jobs. Government paper work is often so pervasive that it requires that the real-life

125

programs be altered to make it easy to account for and explain them. Without it, the program predominates and paper work is used only to assist in the effective completion of the program.

2. The possibilities of audit, disallowance, and the general attitude of government investigators that everybody who takes government funds is to be viewed with suspicion can militate against not only the government but the program, and ultimately against the black beneficiary.

3. In the event of jobs which require only nominal amounts of induction and training, such as semiskilled operative positions, there would be no necessity for government aid, since often the disadvantaged employee, particularly the ex-convict or the drop-out, may have a high enough native intelligence to acquire the skills required without special treatment beyond what any new employee would require.

Other firms will find that in Figure 4 they would locate themselves in the category 7 to 8. This range would consist of policies supporting programs such as job corps camps, where the OEO has sought industrial bidders to provide managerial and logistic know-how on a contract basis. Here the contractor takes on as an additional business activity the staffing and management of a new enterprise. Watts Manufacturing would be one example of a company that has done this, and systems engineering companies who apply systems engineering to the cities on contract would be another. The reasons for this policy position would be as follows:

1. The poverty industry, like space and defense, is a

legitimate area for private enterprise to compete in. While the profits are generally circumscribed, this kind of contracting is no worse than other contracting for the government, and provides a needed service at efficient prices. The discipline of private profit is brought to bear on social problems.

2. For industries where cutbacks have occurred, the policy provides continued employment for high-talent people who might otherwise be thrown on the job market by contract cancellations and program cutbacks. This could depress certain areas such as the hometowns of the aerospace and systems businesses in Southern California.

3. The private firm which enters the poverty market as a business has a commitment to its employees and stockholders, and will be aggressive and innovative in seeking out fruitful areas of service, and ingenious in executing its plans. It will be free from many of the political persuasions that sometimes accompany governmentally conducted programs.

Other Important Policy Issues

The two basic decisions above—to what extent to seek to employ the disadvantaged, and whether or not to seek government aid—are productive of a general posture toward program objectives. There are more issues. A few of them are listed below. Many will be clarified if, using the same kind of scale (from 1 to 8, with the lower end of the range being more restrictive and the higher end being the most liberal), you assess your company's policy position at the present time and make a conscientious choice.

- How strong a position should the large corporation take in encouraging suppliers to employ and train the disadvantaged? Many large firms have thousands of suppliers, and while enforcement may not be possible or even legal, the buyer has the privilege of stating his opinions to vendors, who may accept them or not.
- How strong a position should a company take upon discrimination in the life of the community around it? U.S. Steel has been criticized for not using its muscle in Birmingham politics, for example. Ford Motor Company, a clear leader in employment, is located in Dearborn, Mich., where not a single black family resides.
- Should a firm relocate or even remain in an urban site where taxes and city services are deteriorating, when it could move to a more suitable economic location outside the city?
- How much executive and staff time should be allocated to the problems of the urban crisis? Should a firm have a complete staff, and loan employees to poverty programs, or should it be silent and permit employees to do what they feel like doing on their own time, or even forbid such activity?

Converting Policy into Practice

The definition of policy is a guide to action. It subse-

128

quently converts into procedures, practices, and regulations. After the policy has been clarified, and only then, are the operating managers able to move freely to execute the policy. The execution is the remaining frontier.

Once supervision is assured that a policy really *is* a policy and top management *really means it,* then changed procedures and supervisory practices will follow. Most supervisors, general foremen, and plant managers, once convinced, are then ready for some completed staff work which answers the question, "Okay, so I'm convinced, but how do I do it and make it work?"

10

MIDDLE MANAGEMENT PROGRAMS

It is a long step from saying the truth to
doing it.

> Cervantes,
> DON QUIXOTE

Clarence Randall, former chairman of Inland Steel, once noted that the top position in the firm is a lonely one. Often the top man is isolated from the mass of opinion, and from the problems of people several levels down. This is never made more apparent than when top management catches fire on some issue such as civil rights, or changing employment standards, and finds itself running into a massive bank of inertia. The common idea that all top management's wishes become self-executing orders is, of course, fiction. It is a fiction which the lower levels of management itself help perpetuate by verbally conceding the authority of the top, while in fact they are dragging their feet.

There is a certain amount of wisdom which organizations develop in the face of campaigns. Perhaps "This too shall pass" is a realistic response to top management fads, which the isolated top man is prone to bring back from meetings. Under the persuasive sway of an orator at a conference for top management, it is not uncommon for the

"Old Man" to come back with a flash of inspiration, which may or may not last. Thus, the response to a campaign of allowing the dust to settle can be characterized as normal in most sizable organizations.

What are the requirements of top management, and what are some effective instruments that can be applied to the middle management group in order to move the organization in the direction of making things happen? Presuming that the policy has been clarified and uttered, what else is required? Four major actions affecting the middle management seem to be involved.

1. The policy statement is issued with a fairly clear *statement of objectives* for the program.
2. Resources are assigned or released to implement the program, so that *organization for action* is permitted to occur.
3. Specific *plans and programs* are requested, and are approved by the major chiefs of departments and divisions. In the instance of civil rights programs, these seem to involve more than an ordinary amount of *training*.
4. *Control and feedback machinery* is established to assure compliance, and the results are made part of the performance assessment of subordinate managers.

Statements of Objectives

Henry Ford II, speaking in Washington in August 1967 to the Urban Coalition convocation, laid down the pattern not only for the delegates, but for action by his own middle managers.

131

The primary contribution of business is to provide genuinely equal opportunities for employment, training and promotion. Much has been done along these lines, but much remains to be done—both by business and by those unions that still restrict membership on the basis of race. . . .

Even more basic than the responsibility of business to provide equal jobs is the responsibility to stay in business so that it can provide jobs. No business can survive if it neglects the axioms of sound management. Business cannot hire more people than it needs, or hire people who are not qualified to do useful work, or hire people for more than their work is worth. This means that the key to equal employment opportunity is vastly expanded and improved education and training for those who now receive the least and poorest preparation for a productive life. . . .

Some may feel it unseemly to mention cost and profit when urgent human needs are involved. The profit motive is a powerful force. It must be maintained, and it can be used effectively to help solve the urban crisis. This is not, however, a justification for business as usual. These are unusual times and they demand unusual efforts and unusual sacrifice from every individual and organization that has the power to help.

The guidelines here show the limiting conditions under which the middle manager must work. (a) He must continue to be a successful operator with respect to production, quality, safety, spoilage, waste, turnover, absenteeism, sales, service, costs, and protection of assets. (b) He must add another objective, of hiring people previously considered unemployable, and integrate them into the work force. (c) The vehicle by which this is to be done is primarily through an expanded training effort at every level of the organization.

132

Organization for Action

As indicated by Figure 5, organization for action in a large company is a flow of policy and objectives downward and a flow back up of programs and procedure. For such a program to be developed at all will require special staff experts, often located in the employee or industrial relations department, to devise and promulgate such action. The two phases shown in such a program affecting middle management are as follows:

1. *A specific communication in writing* to plant managers and other key executives by the officer in charge of each division, staff department, or major activity reinforcing the company commitment, and directing three major steps:

(a) That plant managers and other major unit leaders meet with plant managerial and supervisory personnel, and give personal endorsement of the program of accelerated hiring, at the same time explaining the limitations and objectives which must be met concurrently with the new objectives.

(b) That each plant manager develop a plan and submit it by a specific time for filing and general approval, and that it assign a local staff person to be responsible for it. This makes clear an individual managerial commitment to specific results sought.

(c) That each plant or major unit leader spell out how the results to which the subordinate manager commits himself will be reflected in such matters as pay, promotion, performance recording, bonus, and future assignments of the subordinate manager.

133

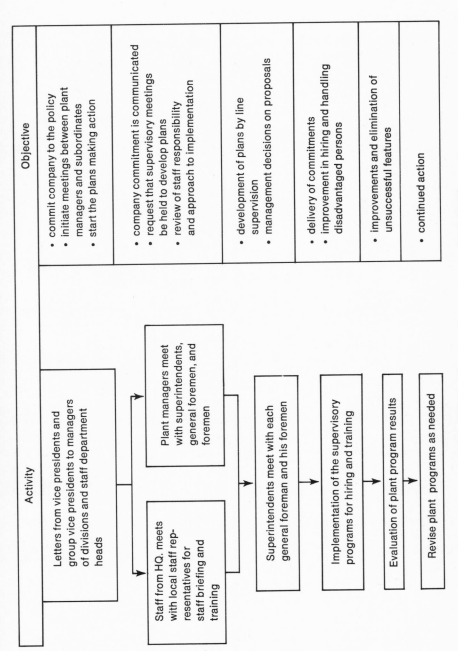

FIGURE 5. Developing plans for hiring the culturally disadvantaged.

2. Two sets of meetings should be held simultaneously. The first is between plant managers and all of their major subordinates, including superintendents, general foremen, and foremen. At the same time the central staff department responsible for the staff work on the urban affairs program should hold meetings with a designated staff equivalent assigned in each plant to implement the corporate programs.

(a) *In the line management meetings* the topics should be a firm statement of the commitment of the company, and the upward commitment of subordinate supervision to the achievement of specific objectives in employing the disadvantaged.

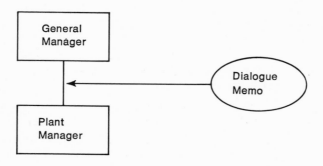

FIGURE 6.
The commitment process.

Figure 6 shows the nature of the commitment process between superior and subordinate managers at the middle manager level. The mechanical devices of a dialogue to discuss objectives in this area and confirming memos in documentation comprise the fabric of a commitment. Commit-

135

ment here is that which is woven into the basic responsibility of the manager. Thus, hiring the disadvantaged is not an additional program, but part of that basic responsibility.

> **The subordinate middle manager who makes a commitment to achieve a result is practically obliged to try his best to achieve it. The superior in turn is obliged as a practical matter to use results achieved as a criteria in measuring that manager's performance.**

(b) *In the staff meeting* between the corporate headquarters staff and the assigned staff man from the plant or division, procedures and standards for acceptable staff work for the local "Manager of Urban Affairs" are spelled out.

- *Staff work* previously completed by the central staff is distributed and explained, and suggestions are solicited.
- The general categories of *advice, service,* and *control* comprise the major outputs of staff departments. The local plant staff man, often the industrial relations man or a man especially assigned to the task (many choose blacks for this position) must understand that he reports to the local manager, who pays his salary, at the same time that he is armed with assistance, materials, advice, and technical backup by the central staff. Suggested procedures are proposed, in which it is important to include systems of feeding back results and problems to a central coordinating body.
- *Procedures for upward communications* of problems, especially of supervisors in the local plant, are spelled out, and dissemination of the solutions of those problems to all local staff coordinators is planned. Newsletters, memos, or bulletins on a regular basis can be issued to keep all staff coordinators abreast of what problems others are having, and what solutions have worked.

136

- *Trade-off goals* should be clearly specified. As one large company instructed its plant coordinators, "You will be expected to show steady progress in hiring the disadvantaged. At the same time you must not trade away your absenteeism and turnover figures in the process. *Both* are your concern." If the trade-offs seem self-canceling or even impossible, it is better to spell them out in advance than to be silent about them, only to complain later that they weren't achieved.
- *Special requirements or special programs,* such as a JOBS program which is being planned at the central staff level, comprise another suitable topic of discussion. The major requirement here is that the local staff coordinator know clearly what his responsibilities in each such program might be, and what would constitute good or bad results.

Specific Plans and Programs

In moving into a new and untested area such as hiring the disadvantaged, the planning and programming of *method* should begin at the lower levels of the organization. Figure 7 shows the specific flow of information which is required.

The flow downward consists of definition of objectives, statements of policy, authorization for use of resources, and information. The upward flow consists of statements of detailed plans, methods of achievement proposed, procedures adopted, reports of results, and definition of specific problems found in application.

The end effect of this exchange will in more instances than not produce a vast surge in training at the lower levels,

137

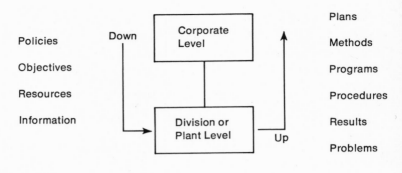

FIGURE 7.

which suggests that the local coordinator might in many instances be a training expert. The specific details of the training, its content and method, and the assessment of results for such training are discussed in the next chapter.

The effects of different types of participation and the choice of media and procedures may mean that varying methods will be used in different locations. This variety is not without merit.

1. If plants are allowed to vary their approaches as they see the necessity on the scene, more innovation and ingenuity is apt to occur. By a system of reports to a central coordinating agency, all involved staff plants can share in the pooled experience of other plants.

2. Allowing for variation removes the central staff from the untenable position of being required to become the all-purpose expert on local matters in every plant. Their expertness emerges rather from their strategic position, from which they can see the efforts of all the various local

138

groups, and an ability to communicate general principles as they observe them. Variety also assists them in solving problem areas, since they have access to the best practices of all; should a local plant fall down in executing a program, or fail to develop a sensible one, the central staff department can bring the cumulative experience of other, more successful programs to bear on the specific plant's failures. In some instances this action will consist of visits and consultation. In others it will be a simple referral: "Why don't you go over and visit Jim in the Foundry. He had that problem and licked it. Go talk to him."

3. It removes the onus of "top down" enforcement, which tends to generate resistance among local managers. The local manager who feels that he is being shoved into actions inconsistent with local conditions, or ones that don't take competing influences such as production or labor relations into account, may consciously or unconsciously drag his feet in making the program work. If he devises his own program and is permitted to modify it as needed, yet receives help when he wants it, this ill effect is allayed.

4. Variety generates a healthy air of competition among local managers and staff people, who see that their own ingenuity and vigor in executing programs will redound to their benefit, and conceive a desire to excel in this matter of hiring along with all others.

Control and Reporting Systems

Attempting to conduct a program for a large corporation

on a centralized basis, or attempting to enforce a foolish consistency, will only cause the program to falter. What then are the purposes of control?

The major control is a firmly enforced rule that the option to DO NOTHING is not open to any division, plant, or major unit.

The specific details are to be prepared and submitted by the local unit within a specified time. If they are not forthcoming after appropriate reminder, the authority of the line is invoked through notification of the higher levels of management that the division is in noncompliance with policy.

The division or plant which submits a seemingly workable plan is autonomous to execute its own plans as it has stated its intentions to do.

The division or plant which submits no plan or an inadequate plan is subjected to somewhat more control. The plan may be rejected, for example, with the statement that others have done more, and with some suggestions for improvement.

The division or plant which flatly refuses to submit plans is subject to corporate muscle. The ordinary devices of pay increases, performance reports, bonuses, and the like are all available and well known. These of course are extremely unlikely to be required, since middle managers are not unaware of their potential application.

A large southern plant of a northern corporation received a directive to move quickly on integration and hiring the disadvantaged. The plant manager read the memo to his staff. There followed a dull silence. "Suppose we don't do it?" asked one of the superintendents. "Then report to the cashier. He'll have your pay ready," was the cool reply. "Do we have to like it?" inquired another. "Nope, we just have to do it well," replied the plant manager. The program worked admirably without a hitch.

Not "Should We?" But "How Do We?"

The use of participative management in integrating a plant has some potential dangers which should be noted.

The lower levels of management may have some deep-rooted beliefs and personal feelings which militate against their acceptance of the idea at all. To flush these into the open and crystallize them will cause nothing but delay, unnecessary squabbling, and ineffective programs. If they become even partially convinced that they are being asked *whether or not* the urban affairs program is a good thing they will naturally try to drag their feet and will develop some highly effective resistance. Such resistance can be avoided by a simple rule, rigidly enforced.

Never ask subordinates what they think of the policy. Tell them that the policy is a must, and that questions about its wisdom are not being asked. The best methods of implementing it, however, are things in which they are being asked to participate.

141

11

RESPONSIBILITIES OF THE FOREMAN

The Buck stops here.
President Harry S. Truman

While some significant gains have been made in office oc-cupations, for the most part the hard-core unemployed and underemployed have been located in factory positions. Under such circumstances, it becomes apparent that the foreman and general foreman must assume heavy respon-sibilities for making the program work.

The preceding pages have made it clear that top man-agement must first make it crystal clear that they want such a program, that no debate on the merits of the policy is on the agenda. It now falls to the foreman, working with the instruction and support of his immediate boss (usually called the general foreman) to devise immediate day-to-day plans and make them work.

Introducing the Subject to Management on the Floor

Cold memos and directives will clearly not get the job

done. The word must be passed, and the plant superintendent, after being briefed by the plant manager, should conduct an individual meeting with each of the major clusterings of plant supervisors. Here the procedures become clear.

1. The superintendent for each area conducts a series of meetings attended by a general foreman and all of the foremen reporting to him. His personal attendance at all sessions is important to indicate his personal interest in the success of the program.

2. The industrial relations manager or local urban affairs staff man schedules the meeting, provides the instructional materials, and if necessary briefs the leaders on what to cover.

3. The plant manager may very well make the introductory remarks for each meeting, reading company statements of policy, and lending personal endorsement to the program.

4. The meetings should be held in the best available executive conference room. If there is a suitable conference space in the plant manager's office, or if there is a board room, holding the meeting there will emphasize its importance. Tailgate sessions or overturned-box conferences on the plant floor are less desirable than an up-front session.

5. It is advisable to get a written notice of the meeting to people several days in advance, indicating the importance of the session and urging a clearing of the decks for it.

6. Several days before the meeting, the staff man in

143

charge should meet with all who will be taking part to pre-
pare an agenda, go over the content, and possibly rehearse
before the first session.

7. Visual aids should be planned and tried out before the
meeting. One large company borrowed a series of films
comprised of footage from newsreels, made into video
tape to run on a sixteen millimeter sound projector, showing scenes from some recent riots and disorders not far
from the plant. Your public relations department should
be able to arrange for borrowing or buying such footage.
Films or slides, or possibly tapes of important individuals
stressing the urgency of the problem, can also affect attitudes toward the problem. Occasionally city or state police
have films in their files which they will lend upon request.

8. Where discussion sessions are planned, the superintendent and general foreman should serve as coleaders.
Notes of all discussions should be made and copies distributed to the foreman. This can be done by the staff man
who attends as an observer.

How a Typical Meeting Might Go

Visits to a number of plants where foremen are being
introduced to the subject would indicate that there are
some major requirements for successfully carrying off such
a session.

1. *Read a copy of the company policy* where it is available. If the chairman or president has written or said any-

thing which would be evidence of his determination to press on in hiring the disadvantaged, read it and distribute copies. In one company each member of the group was given a personal copy of the Kerner Commission Report to read before coming.

2. *Review the meeting held by the plant manager* with his superintendents. If he has issued a plant policy statement and statements of local objectives, present these as well. Four areas should be covered:

a. Make it clear that the company is committed to hiring the unemployed and adhering to the principle of equal opportunity.
b. Spell out the trade-off objectives, so that everyone understands that production, quality, housekeeping, safety, low absenteeism, and low turnover must also be achieved.
c. Stress the importance of good treatment of the new employee by fellow employees and foremen.
d. Point to the need for special effort to make the program work, and the fact that this program becomes a measurable part of the supervisor's responsibilities.

3. *Stress the three major areas* in which foremen will probably be affected by the new program: induction, job instruction training, and special actions and programs.

First, the foreman will be called upon to do an even better job of *inducting* new employees than he has done in the past. At this stage, if the company has a good program for inducting new employees the details should be reviewed. Ford, for example, has a small wallet-card checklist reviewed in the company's foreman training session on managing the disadvantaged new employee. Figure 8 shows the basic outline of an induction program. Such an

145

outline could be printed on a wallet-sized card and distributed at the meeting, or included in handout materials. The

I How to Induct a New Employee in the Plant Department:	II Be Prepared For These Questions:
Introduce yourself.	What time do we . . . • start work • quit work
Welcome employee to department.	• take a break • wash up
Tell him what his department does.	• eat lunch
Explain the rules and regulations: • regular attendance • promptness • safety rules • medical facilities • probationary status • discipline procedures	Where is the . . . • lavatory • cafeteria • time clock • locker room • tool crib • first aid room • water fountain • bulletin board
Explain promotional opportunities.	How do I . . .
Answer his questions until they are all answered.	• punch in and out • get my pay • report in sick • get a shop steward • get emergency relief

FIGURE 8.
Suggested outline for a new-employee-induction program.

foreman will be called upon to do an even better job than in the past of applying the instructions. Often the ordinary new employee has worked in other plants and has some knowledge that such procedures exist. In the case of the disadvantaged worker, *more patience* is required with what might seem to be obvious details.

A second major way the foreman's job will be affected

under the new program will be in more systematic job instruction training of the new worker. Where the foreman himself does the initial job instruction, he may want to review the JIT formula in Figure 9. Devised for training new

I How to Get Ready to Instruct:	II How to Instruct:
Have a time table. How much skill do you expect him to have, in what time? Break the job down. List the important steps. Pick out key points (anything that could make or break the job). Have everything ready to teach. Set up proper equipment, tools, and supplies ahead of time. Have the workplace arranged. It should be just as the worker will be expected to maintain it. If the learner hasn't learned, the teacher hasn't taught.	Step I. Prepare the worker. • put him at ease. • state the job and find out what he already knows about it. • get him interested in learning. • place him in the correct position. Step II. Present the job. • show, tell, and demonstrate each step, one at a time. • stress each key point and have him repeat it back to you. • teach him slowly and patiently until you know that he knows. • don't teach more than he can master at one time. Step III. Performance try-out. • have him do the job; correct his errors. • have him state key points. • answer questions. • continue until you know that he knows. Step IV. Follow-up. • put him on his own. • tell him where to go for help. • check frequently and encourage. • taper off with extra coaching.

FIGURE 9.
Job instruction training.

workers in defense plants during World War I, the formula was used extensively during World War II to train foremen to teach workers factory jobs rapidly under wartime pressures. Over 13 million workers received training under this plan, and it works.

If the foreman has a fairly sizable crew and a training operator, it will be necessary for him to conduct a review session for these trainers to be sure they are following the procedure. The foreman should plan to tackle a couple of job instruction assignments himself. Thus he will be able to see at first hand the problems his job instructors face with the incoming new worker. Regular conferences with the job instructors should be held to note any special problems that are arising. These should be noted on paper and fed back to the plant training department and urban affairs staff man. If problems arise which the foreman cannot cope with he should seek advice immediately.

A third way in which the foreman's job might be affected by a program to employ the disadvantaged is in *special actions* for which he is responsible, and which grow out of the type of new employee he is getting. These will vary from company to company and also according to which functions are to be done by the industrial relations department and which by the foreman. Some companies have added these programs to the foreman's responsibilities:

1. Arrangements for *car pools* and other transportation arrangements, such as bus tickets for employees until they get their first pay check.
2. *Cash advances* against the first pay check, usually two weeks ahead, for lunches.

148

3. Finding a *fellow worker as a buddy* or sponsor during his early weeks in the department.
4. *Attendance at any training courses* conducted by the company for disadvantaged new employees.
5. *The solution to problems* as they arise, and suggestions for special programs to make the program work.

It is in this third area that open discussion should be the rule of the day. Even on the induction program and the JIT program there should be ample opportunity for the foreman to ask questions, and to make suggestions about how the program could be modified or done better. Foremen might foresee problems which will arise in their own areas and which are special to them. These should be discussed, and solutions sought from the group. Also, any programs which they see as helpful in hiring and retaining people and at the same time achieving company and departmental goals should be aired, and notes made of them for subsequent distribution.

Some companies, for example, have telephone calling programs which foremen execute from their own desks. If an employee is absent the foreman calls him, tells him he is missed, and asks the reasons for this absenteeism, and when he will be in. In other companies this wouldn't work; a foreman will say, "My joint is far too noisy," or telephones are not readily available for outside calls without undue delays. In such cases a report of the absentee is sent to the Industrial Relations Department and a member of that staff calls, with a report back to the foreman. In other instances a buddy calls.

149

The idea of getting the foreman involved is twofold. It will bring forth a range of new and imaginative ideas which the staff couldn't develop, not being on the scene. It will also give the foreman more of a sense of involvement in making the program work.

Following Through on the Foreman's Performance

After the introductory meeting, further follow-up meetings may be required. Foremen who have never had JIT training should be enrolled in a special course in that area. A foreman's notebook, into which he puts minutes of meetings and ideas and memos from the civil rights program of the plant, could be distributed and maintained.

Ideas suggested by foremen which are not in their own scope of authority should be processed rapidly when they are submitted for approval. Delayed responses not only set back the idea, but stifle further submissions.

Problem-centered discussions by the general foreman with his foremen should take place at regular intervals. This should concentrate on such practical problems as these:

- How to sell an unwanted job.
- Handling the absentee problem.
- Reducing turnover.
- Reducing resistance of workers to new employees.
- Overcoming limitations upon effective training of new workers.
- Teaching the more complex parts of the job.

150

These can often be handled effectively through "chalk talks," in which the conference leader uses a format along the lines shown in Figure 10.

The Problem
(write the problem in the center top of
the board or chart pad.)

Causes   Possible   Solutions
(Draw lists of causes   (List the possible solutions which
from the foremen.)   are suggested by the group.)

FIGURE 10.

One advantage of using chart paper is that the charts can subsequently be given to a typist and the minutes of the session typed up and distributed to those attending.

Foremen who contribute to the success of the program should have this fact acknowledged in several ways. They should receive verbal and perhaps written congratulations from general foremen, or from higher up if the contributions are especially good. Praise is probably more effective when it is done by a superior in the presence of other foremen. His achievements should also be noted in his annual performance review, and reflected in merit increases in salary. In some firms management suggestion systems make it possible to achieve significant cash awards for ideas of merit. Competition among foremen in retention of former hard-core unemployed could lead to awards for those who exceed desired levels.

151

What Are the Problems the Foreman Faces?

In taking on new responsibility for hiring and handling disadvantaged people, the company is handing the foreman a new set of problems, and should be ready to recognize this, and provide the backing, staff support, and understanding needed.

Larry Washington, a black man, is a veteran industrial relations manager in Ford's Engine and Foundry Division now promoted to the corporate Equal Opportunity Office at headquarters. He reports that his experience with thousands of such employees processed through his shop shows a definitive pattern of problems which can be expected, though not all occur in all places. Washington lists eight possible problems, projects a couple for the future, and tells what has happened with them at Ford. He reports that "there are really none of them that large doses of human understanding and compassion can't solve." The eight major ones he lists follow.

Eight Major Problems Supervisors Report in
On-the-Job Supervision of Hard-Core Unemployed

1. The primary problem is instilling dependability and getting the people to show up every day on time. Very often the hard-core unemployed believe that a job at Ford is similar in kind to the jobs they had as car washers or brochure handlers. "I am not taking any money when I am not

152

in, so why should the company worry?" The idea that the company *needs the employee* regularly and that his absence causes difficulties for the supervisor who counts on the employees to staff his production operation is hard to put across.

2. Job performance, once they have been on the job and after job instruction training, has not been a problem. Their performance is as good as the average Ford employee, and their output is up to standard.

3. Inability to read signs, inability to distinguish safety directions, and so on have constituted no great problem. Of the 5,000 employees in the hard-core group hired at Ford, only three or four illiterates have been discovered at the point of employment. Even here, the overcoming of the illiteracy to bring them up to a functional level where they could operate successfully has not been a serious problem.

4. There has been no counterreaction among white employees and certainly none on an organized basis. There are a few people who may resent the hiring of the hard-core unemployed but they generally show their feeling by *withholding assistance* or cooperation that might have been extended to someone with whom they had positive friendly relations. Resentment where it exists does not take the form of any positive hazing, harassment, or interference that demonstrates itself in open criticism. The principal attitude of the white employee on the assembly line or the factory floor is "How does this affect *me*?" If it doesn't have a substantial effect on him in terms of his having to work harder to make up for the newcomers' shortcomings, he shows no resentment.

153

5. In the area of union relations, the union has been extremely cooperative. In fact our union shop agreement requires payment of union dues. The new employees are treated well by members of the union. They get the kind of treatment that any union member would get.

6. Turnover records compare quite favorably with those of other employees hired in the last three or four years. Of course, during that period the Great Lakes area has had a great labor shortage, so lots of marginal people have been hired. Nonetheless the hard-core group does compare favorably and comprises no major serious problem for the supervisor.

7. As for supervision problems, the general feeling is that supervisors "can live with it." There have been no changes in the ratio of supervision to employees, and no special efforts on the job have been made. Perhaps the major effect has been that the standard company orientation which has always been prescribed for new employees now is apt to get a more complete and full treatment than it had in the past. This doesn't mean that the company regulations are amended or that company practices have changed, but merely that they are more fully applied. All management personnel and all manufacturing supervisors are put through a preparation session in which the principal subject matter taught is covered in a booklet, "Helping the New Hourly Employee Succeed on the Job."

8. Plans for the future include demonstration training programs for hiring and training hard-core unemployed persons. Jobs are provided for men and women on welfare, high school drop-outs, prison parolees, and persons

who quit after being hired as part of the company's present inner city recruiting program. Some of the enrollees are unable to read or write. Under the plan Ford determines the kinds of education, training, and counseling needed to help them become productive employees. The plan is identified as Operation 250, because 250 persons will be hired under Government Program MA-3. The results have been most favorable to date and will be expanded. Under MA-3 any employer may apply for assistance from the United States Department of Labor in the form of grants to cover losses incurred during the training period for hard-core unemployed.

Will the Whole Thing Work?

There's enough evidence at hand already to demonstrate clearly that hiring and keeping the disadvantaged can be done. The eight problems listed by Mr. Washington were circulated to thirty other industrial relations managers in companies which had programs, none as extensive as Ford's. They all agreed in substance, with some special local circumstances as the basis for variations from Ford's basic list.

This means that many of the selection instruments relied upon in the past simply weren't valid. Felix Lopez, selection expert for The Port of New York Authority, reported in *Personnel Psychology* on that organization's experience in hiring toll collectors. A number of applicants who flunked

155

the tests and ordinarily would have been rejected were hired—and subsequently succeeded.

In a study of selection processes and a follow-up on their effects, two West Coast psychologists reported in *Personnel Psychology* in 1968[1] that on a sample of over 1,000 applicants the Wonderlic test didn't predict success of blacks. The authors said that well-conducted interviews plus a weighted application blank seemed to work better. They also found that the turnover rate among blacks was from 10 to 20 percent less than for whites after the first ten weeks of employment. A partial explanation is that black employees simply have fewer job opportunities, and therefore are more apt to stick with a job than whites. This, of course, has been the experience of disadvantaged employees of other types, such as the physically handicapped.

The practical evidence, coupled with other evidence from research, indicates that such programs can be made to work. Many firms that are doing their best are still reluctant to discuss their results, until the findings are more final. Yet, the experience of those who have tried to solve this terrible social problem through using the resources of private enterprise have shown that at the operating level the approach poses no insuperable problems.

Despite the fact that there is no alternative, and that the evidence shows that it can be done, there are still those who haven't seen the flames and moved. They may run out of time.

12

THE ROCKY ROAD
AHEAD

When large numbers of people cannot
find work, the result is unemployment.
                    Calvin Coolidge

One of the more worrisome features of the employment
drive which has been such a success where it has been
tried, is the specter of a recession which would require that
people newly hired and trained be discharged. Arthur Ross,
former Commissioner of Labor Statistics for the U.S. Department of Labor, in a parting interview prior to becoming
a vice president of the University of Michigan, touched on
this possibility and its consequences.

He predicted that the additional tax surcharge enacted
in 1968, coupled with a $6 billion budget cut, would pro-
duce a cutback in employment. "My own guess would be
that by the end of the year the overall rate would be in the
neighborhood of four percent," he said. He went on to state
that it might move "in the direction of four and a half percent," in the first half of 1969. The unemployment rate at
the time of his prediction was 3.5 percent. The predicted
rate would also produce a cutback in hours worked per

week, and fewer women and children would be in the work force. A rate reaching 4.5 percent unemployed "is going to be particularly hard on those hard-core unemployed who have been pulled into industry through government programs." This, he indicated, would be because seniority systems will require that the newly hired be released first, including the ghetto residents.

The possibility of such cutbacks constitutes an important problem for business and the general peace and stability of the city. As Henry Ford II put it in the *Michigan Business Review* in 1968,

> Securing job pledges is only the beginning of what we must do. This program will fail unless the people who are hired become permanent, productive members of the labor force. It is not a relief program or a make-work program, or a gimmick to cool things for the summer. Our efforts will do harm, not good, if we hire people, raise their hopes, and let them slide back into idleness and despair.

Hedges Against Depression

The possibility of a full-dress depression is not a major concern today. Nonetheless the possibility of unemployment becomes an urgent agenda item during the period of early employment for the hard-core unemployed. It takes a couple of years for a new employee to build up seniority and supplemental benefit credits to ease the shock of sudden unemployment upon this newly employed group. Sev-

158

eral kinds of hedges are possible against such a harmful stimulant to civil disorder as raising and then dashing people's aspirations.

1. *A general program of upgrading the skills level* of every employee who has the capacity to be trained can be conducted on an accelerated basis. The funds for MDTA and other programs to speed up training of the hard core for higher-level positions can be applied more quickly.

2. *Union relations* can encompass some hard bargaining, of which there has been a rather sparse amount in recent years, pressing unions to ease those restrictive practices that work hardship on the newly hired hard-core unemployed.

3. *Federal, state, and local governments* could be much more diligent in applying internally to their own employment practices the kinds of procedures that they so vigorously and sanctimoniously enforce upon private sector employers. Present practices of "testing as usual" are in fact a means of implementing business and discrimination as usual in governmental employment.

4. *General snubbers for downturns of the economy* can be used to offset the undesirable effects which Dr. Ross predicted would ensue from the tax increase and budget cut.

Let's look at each of these possibilities further.

Upgrading Skills Levels

A common quip in many large organizations when the

president or board chairman is retired is, "Well, eventually they'll have to hire a new janitor." This comment implies that, by a promotion-from-within policy, when the president retires a vice president moves up, thus leaving a vacancy to be filled by a department head, who in turn vacates a position to be filled by a lesser rank.

The rationale behind this progression poses a serious danger of locking the hard-core unemployed in the labor force.

Figure 11 illustrates the stair-step plan of job succession for a typical factory work force. Labor grades among

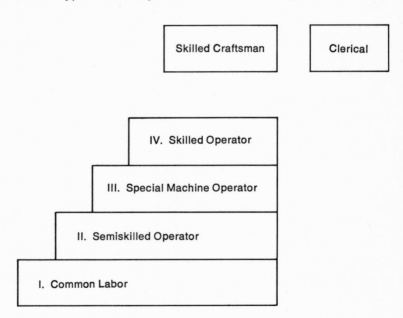

FIGURE 11.
The hierarchy of hourly labor.

160

hourly workers will typically consist of four or five, from common laborer to the first of the skilled trades such as machinist, millwright, pipefitter, rigger, electrician, carpenter, tool and diemaker, and the like.

Ordinarily in a labor market with such a work force, the first to be released are in the lowest labor category, since these are ordinarily the newest workers, and their level of skill is the least likely to be needed when production cutbacks are required by market decline. The higher labor grades will probably be required to accept a "bump" back to a lower classification, but in a declining job market this is preferable to unemployment, and it is provided for in labor agreements.

Since promotion in the lowest four labor grades in large unionized plants is ordinarily done on the basis of seniority, the raising of a worker from grade I to grade II will not necessarily protect his employment rights very significantly unless at the same time he has built up seniority on the company payroll. Thus, a laborer grade III with low seniority would be released or laid off before a higher-seniority laborer grade I, if such a ranking were possible at all.

An employee entering the skilled trades, however, ordinarily finds a system of seniority prevailing for that class of employee alone. His tenure is more certain for several reasons. For one thing skilled employees are more apt to be retained during a layoff, since in many cases their skills will be needed if the plant is to function at all. Companies also have a tendency to hang on to their skilled work force, since these employees are harder to come by in today's labor market. If the cutback in market appears to be short-

161

lived, the tendency of plant management to shift such skilled people into construction, repair and overhaul, or other kinds of work is higher than in the event of reduced production, where the first labor grades will be released or furloughed as quickly as the cutback is noted. A plant on two shifts, for example, will immediately lay off the entire production operator crew with low seniority, transferring the skilled men—who have both skill and seniority going for them—onto other work on the day shift.

This means that the journeyman, who has served an apprenticeship and enjoys a skilled rating, has preferential standing in the labor market. Even where a company finds business sufficiently bad that it must lay off mechanics, pipefitters, and so on, they ordinarily have little trouble finding suitable work in other companies which have not been affected by a recession. Even in the depths of the great depression, a skilled tool and diemaker or machinist was seldom out of work for any length of time. If Detroit was depressed he could always travel and follow his trade in Minneapolis or San Francisco. His skills being widely sought and his pay high, almost equal to that of lower levels of management in many instances, his ability to finance movement was possible.

One of the important steps required to avoid the bumps on the rocky road in private employment is the opening of more apprenticeship opportunities for entry of blacks into the skilled trades.

Theodore Kheel, New York City's labor relations expert, has pointed out the extent of discrimination in the skilled trades, particularly where the skilled trade is organized by craft unions. Black men, he notes, constitute only 15 of every 1,000 electricians in the U.S. and 33 of every 1,000 pipefitters and plumbers. Of 5,658 skilled workers employed on major federal construction projects, a 1963 survey showed that 300 were black: a ratio of 1 to 19. Among 65 major industrial corporations under Plans for Progress, black workers filled about 2½ percent of the skilled craft jobs.[1]

The percentage of the work force that has gained entry into skilled occupations has risen steadily since 1951. Yet, even such skilled people are more apt to be unemployed if they are black than if they are white. The same is true of the white collar occupations, especially clerical positions. The number of black managers has risen very slowly in the past ten years. The number of black salesmen has risen more rapidly, in part because of the recognition of the black market and because the ability of blacks to sell to blacks is superior to that of whites.

To be unemployed is always unfortunate, no matter what your race. If, however, a proportionate share of qualified black workers could be upgraded into skilled positions, and into white collar occupations of a technical, managerial, or sales nature, the benefits would be high and the penalties equalized in good times and bad. In good times it would mean that positions now occupied by black employees would be vacated if the present incumbents were trained to assume higher-level skilled jobs. By underemployment the qualified black man works below his potential. In working there he blocks the even less qualified black worker from obtaining any position whatsoever. By proper upgrading, the effects of unemployment in bad times would fall more proportionately among the races and would be less likely to produce the results Dr. Ross predicted.

The Unions and the Hard Core

It would be wrong to characterize unions as being a single cause, or even the major one, of black unemployment. It would also be wrong to label all unions as discriminatory. With some exceptions, most of the major industrial unions such as the United Automobile Workers, the USWA (United Steel Workers of America), and the like have been active in fighting racial discrimination in their membership. Mr. Washington's statement on the Ford experience is probably typical of such unions as the Rubber Workers, Steel Workers, Packinghouse Workers, and other industrial unions. The same has not been true of the craft unions, who have had a policy of barring black men from membership in their unions, and thus have the power to keep them from being employed. The unions of craftsmen like plumbers, electricians, and sheet metal workers have traditionally either barred blacks from membership or restricted them to certain kinds of work. In recent years the striking of discriminatory clauses in most union constitutions has occurred and today no more than two or three continue to bar black workers in their formal policy. Fair employment practices laws have outlawed many of these practices, and the National Labor Relations Board has found unions guilty of unfair labor practices in cases where racial quotas existed. The craft unions, however, have a peculiar power under most of their contracts through closed shop agreements and elaborate work rules. The employers agree to call the union for new employees, and these are drawn by the union only from among their membership. Thus, failure to get into the union is a bar to employment.

In industrial unions, Professor Marshall finds, "The union has probably done more to promote than to retard Negro job opportunities."[2] Top international leadership has adopted equalitarian policies, and at the plant level most locals have been vigorous in protecting the rights of black members. In some instances the union has initiated bargaining demands, inserting clauses into the contract assuring nondiscrimination in hiring. In administration of the contract it has not been unknown, however, for the union to overlook its own seniority clauses as they applied to black workers. Often this has been done because the union leadership, which is elected by the membership, has rightly observed that to be overly equalitarian would result in its defeat in the next election.

The Conservative Working Man

The leaders of many unions are faced with a special

165

problem when it comes to energetically pressing for equal opportunity for black workers. The white membership is by and large still some distance behind the leader and heading the other way. Making upward of $7,500 in over half the cases, the unionized worker has become a bastion of resistance against the progessive policies of his union. Having arrived at a safe plateau where he is relatively free of insecurity in his job, insured against unemployment, and freed from worries about retirement, he is somewhat less than eager to pay the taxes, and suffer the disorders and tensions, which appear to threaten him in the black rise.

This is not true only in his internal plant attitudes and at the union polling place. He has become the main supporter of former Governor George Wallace in the cities, he is the major buyer of guns for personal defense of his property. As A. H. Raskin, veteran labor reporter for *The New York Times,* pointed out, "The working man has become a snob." Writing in *The Saturday Evening Post,* Raskin reported that in the 1967 election, despite an official union endorsement of Beame against Lindsay for mayor of New York City, large numbers of the 150,000 members of the New York teamsters local voted for William Buckley, the ultraconservative candidate who had made it clear that he was against bureaucrats, high taxes, rising welfare rolls, and other things they resented. Raskin cites one trucker:[3]

One teamster official summed it up dolefully after the campaign: "So far as our guys were concerned every candidate but Buckley was a nigger-lover."

166

A truck driver in Michigan said to me that he was opposed to all of the relief and other "handouts" going to blacks. "All they are doing is picking the pockets of the working guy who spent years and sweat blood to get it made, and now they goin' to screw us out of it all with handouts to them cry-baby boogies. I tell you, they ought to work for it like we done."

Louis Harris, the poll-taker, told Raskin that the rank and file of the labor movement are becoming a conservative anchor on the national scene. "On the political front, the workers are way behind the heads of Ford, American Telephone and Telegraph, and other big corporations in their willingness to make room for the people from the slums."

Daniel Moynihan reports surveys which show that workers are "frighteningly" conservative. Interviews conducted by sociologist Gavin McKenzie of Smith College among skilled workers in Providence, R.I., last year showed them out of sympathy with the liberal leanings of their union's leadership.

Liberal Employers and Conservative Workers?

In implementing a policy of hiring the hard-core unemployed, and of upgrading the underemployed, the corporation may expect to obtain the active support of union leadership, at least in the major industrial unions. The possibilities of resistance in this situation are demonstrated in Figure 12.

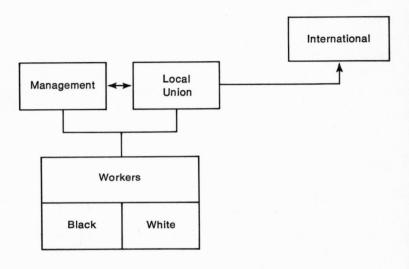

FIGURE 12.

The union officers represent both black workers and white workers, with, in most cases, the whites being a majority. This means that any efforts on the part of management to embellish the status of the black work force will arouse the white segment if they see a threat in such procedures. Faced with insecurity, the white workers will demand that their union represent their will by restricting preferential treatment of blacks. The union officer is then faced with the task of representing a position which his international and perhaps he himself has renounced. If he

168

refuses to represent his members they will unseat him at the next election. If the union leader decides to follow the members' mandate, he will fly against his prior position, against management, and against his international.

From the management viewpoint a tempting opportunity may seem to exist to use the righteous cause of integration to do a little judicious union-busting. The effects of this, however, should be examined. Given a union officer who favors integration but is faced with a conservative membership, it would be no trick to split the union. As a result the union president would lose the next election, and a new, more conservative type would go into office. At this stage, management would be faced with a militant membership and a militant antiblack leadership. In order to make progress in such a climate taking a strike might be necessary in order to carry out any kind of practical preferential treatment in hiring and training, which this book suggests is an alternative to violence.

Management then may find itself confronted with two alternatives, taking a strike, or backing down on hiring black workers. The strike would be preferable for management.

Apart from the obvious fact that management determination to hire black men and train them is the only alternative to violence at a basic level of society, the moral position involved would convert quickly into tactical bargaining strength. A union which struck against hiring or assisting blacks would probably be overwhelmed by public opinion

169

and governmental action if the strike were at all publicized.

The other alternative outcome would be that the international would put the local into the custody of a trustee. The president of an Ohio machine tool firm, whose plant was in the inner city, was asked by his industrial relations manager what he should do in response to union demands that blacks not be "pushed so hard." "The answer is hell, no," he stated. "You have my authorization to take a strike, and we'll go to the radio and press with our story." The union gave in.

With the union, management must assume a strong leadership position, perhaps not by hard-nosed tactics such as the above president prescribes, but a more persuasive yet unflinching sales program to get blacks into jobs on several steps of the ladder, including skilled trades positions.

Government Could Hire More Blacks

A recent directive of the Federal Communications Commission sternly warned companies in the communications field to stop their discriminatory hiring practices. The extent of this discrimination was clearly spelled out in facts and figures. Warnings of forthcoming enforcement measures were spelled out in a model display of government muscle in its regulatory capacity. Clearly this was a needed reform for an industry which has been characterized by bias, discrimination, and a cynicism toward social values

170

which has attracted the attention of business critics and muckrakers for many years. Yet, it was this same stern and righteous agency which had been featured for its own massive efforts at discrimination in an article by Julius Dobson three months before in *The Saturday Evening Post*.[4] The case was not atypical, for at federal, state, and local levels the government is an ominous enforcer of, but a distinctly reluctant participant in, equal employment opportunities for blacks.

The manager of a large midwestern state's personnel department, which employs thousands of persons, did an informal survey of black employees in all state agencies, and found that although it was the largest employer in the state, it had no black employees in any of the three highest grades in seventeen of twenty-one departments. Although the state has a fair employment practices act, it is itself one of the more reluctant employers of blacks. The personnel man reported in a letter to the writer:

> I sent a lengthy letter to the chairman of the state civil service commission pointing out the situation. I pointed out that the testing programs which have been developed over the years were an instrument of discrimination, and that one day soon there would be a blow-up over this government's trailing behind industry in doing the socially right thing. I didn't hear from him at all, until one day I ran into him in the State Office Building and asked him if he had received my letter. He brushed me aside, rather curtly. "Don't make waves, Mr. ——," he said.

The situation is similar, if not worse, at the municipal

level. Most city and county governmental employees, with the possible exception of laborers and others in the lowest labor grades, are white. Black men not only have not been sought out, they have been sufficiently surrounded by culturally biased testing that they would find little chance of being employed if they tried.

If federal, state, and local governments were included as "employers" under the definition of Title VII of the Civil Rights Act of 1964, literally thousands of governmental units would be found in violation of the law. A sampling inspection and query of municipal employers in cities over 10,000 population in Michigan and Ohio tentatively shows that about 95 percent of such cities, especially the small-to medium-size ones, would be in violation of either the federal law or their own state fair employment practices acts. The reason was given by one city manager:

After all, we are here to serve the public and that is the major concern. The quality of our service cannot be allowed to decline. We really do hire every qualified applicant without regard to race or color, but none of the Negroes who apply are qualified.

If the Equal Employment Opportunity Commission were to be granted the power to issue cease and desist orders to government agencies, in the same fashion in which the NLRB issues cease and desist orders in the finding of unfair labor practices for private employers or unions, the practices might be eradicated faster. For private employers, these orders are subject to affirmation orders by the courts.

172

A similar enforcement procedure might be applied to EEOC orders against governmental employers.

The Paucity of Training in Government

With the striking exception of the Defense Department, which is a model governmental employer in terms of integration in hiring, promotion, and training, most governmental agencies are woefully weak in their training effort. Training officers, where they exist at all, are customarily too low in rank, too light in weight, and hobbled by niggardly budgets. Although the typical federal agency has a manager of training, he is usually so limited that drastic curtailment of his activity is common at the first sign of a reduction in force. Often this lack of proper incentive produces an ineffective job holder, frustrated by his inability to make anything happen, and the good ones often find it fruitful to take their talents to private employers. With the exception of the 100 largest cities in the United States, it is extremely unlikely that there will be any individual at all who is responsible for training in the government of our cities. In the absence of such an office, the amount of training done is practically nonexistent. Compare this with General Motors, which has its own accredited college, General Motors Institute, which upgrades General Motors' employees through a bachelor's degree in engineering, business, or science, and has an enrollment in the thousands.

G.M.'s present President, Edward Cole, is a GMI graduate. In addition to this, the typical GM manufacturing plant has a training director and staff of trainers in skills and crafts, as well as a staff for technical and managerial training. A typical state agency in Michigan, which is actually ahead of most states, has a total staff of 2,000 and one full-time training supervisor, who often must wear two hats. But the typical firm, in addition to giving the staff support necessary to train personnel at all levels, budgets substantial sums for tuition refund payments for employees who wish to enroll in courses at evening schools and colleges. Chrysler has an institute somewhat like that at General Motors, and Ford has well-staffed training departments at the corporate, division, and plant levels. The Labor Department, one of the leaders in government, is nonetheless well behind most of *Fortune* magazine's 500 listed companies in staffing and presenting training programs for its employees. Such an environment makes the chance of upgrading negligible, and constitutes a form of *de facto* curtailment of opportunity which should be corrected.

General Measures Against Economic Downturn

Professor Philip Wernette of the University of Michigan has stated the dilemma posed by the urban crisis and the possible disastrous effects of unemployment.[5]

Professor Wernette points out that the 1957–58 slump

174

paradoxically intensified people's concern about inflation. While demand and employment declined, both the wholesale and consumer price indexes continued to rise. This state of affairs flew in the face of the common view that deflation produces unemployment and inflation increases employment. As Wernette put it:

> The situation created this puzzling problem: what medicine to use when the patient has contradictory symptoms, "Dr. Expansion's antideinflationary stimulant" or "Dr. Restraint's anti-inflationary tranquilizer"?

The surtax enacted in 1968 is of a fairly long-run nature, and its effects would not be easily undone if a quick dip were to take place. Does this mean that a harmful dip, which could run unemployment up to 4.5 percent, is possible? While no economist would rule out the possibility, others also point to the short-run "snubbers" that are available to the federal government on almost immediate notice. Arthur Burns has noted some of these, which were applied probably for the first time on any coordinated basis in the recession of 1953.[6] The decline of spending following the Korean War, the buildup of inventories, declining retail sales, and a shorter workweek in manufacturing all pointed to the possibility of a decline.

To offset a possible depression the federal government moved, through the Federal Reserve System, to ease credit by open market purchases and by lowering the rediscount rates on loans to member banks. Accelerated spending of budgeted funds by all departments, heavier spending of government housekeeping funds in the most seriously affected areas, speeding up of Veterans Administration loan procedures, alterations in interest rates to speed up payments of tax rebates, and numerous similar measures were infused into the economy. Burns points out that the private sector was able to muster its latent strength, and the possible serious effects of the downturn were averted.

The point here is that the full resources of the government for short-run application of massive resources to snub a recession must be available on a coordinated, planned basis.

Without such sensitive attention to the problems of recession, the only viable alternative to violence in our cities—jobs provided by corporations—may be undone in a deluge which will produce fire and blood.

APPENDIX

FORD MOTOR COMPANY

January 17, 1968

President
Executive Vice Presidents
Vice Presidents
Group Directors
Division General Managers
Plant Managers
Office Heads
Department Managers
Supervisors, Superintendents and Foremen
Persons Designated by the Above

Equal opportunity is one of Ford Motor Company's
oldest, firmest and most basic policies. The purpose of this
letter is to call on each of you to give that policy your
full and active support, and to put it into practice in
new ways and with a new sense of urgency.

Our goal is to do all we realistically can to give people
who have been held back by prejudice and poverty
a chance to earn a decent life. This goal is entirely
consistent with our responsibility to conduct our business
soundly and profitably. We cannot provide wider

employment opportunities by hiring more people than we need or by keeping people who cannot learn to do their jobs or work with other people. There are, however, many things we can do.

- We can make sure that our requirements for hiring, training and promotion do not exclude able people for irrelevant reasons.

- We can continue to improve our internal training programs and provide leadership and support to public and private community programs to seek out and develop latent abilities that may be productively employed in business and industry.

- We can lend a helping hand in adjusting to the work and the work place, and treat all employees with the dignity and understanding every man owes every other.

- By helping people to help themselves, we can help to cure a social cancer that threatens the vitality and peace of the communities where we do business, to reduce the costs of welfare and crime and the taxes we all pay, and to enlarge the markets for our products.

The Company's Detroit inner-city hiring program is one example of the new approach I am calling for. Its aim is not only to offer employment opportunities, but actively to invite the interest of people who would not normally come to us—not to screen *out* doubtful applicants but to screen *in* if possible—and not merely to hire, but to help them make the grade after they are hired.

I hope that this innovative spirit will be reflected in our personnel policies at every level, and in every other aspect of our business. Opportunities to become a successful Ford dealer or supplier, for example, must be as open and as equal as the opportunities to become a successful employee. And, when we are considering locations for new facilities, we should consider the inner city as well as the suburbs.

I ask each of you to be continuously alert in your own areas for conditions that could obstruct equal opportunity, and to make or suggest changes in the practices that are responsible. I ask each of you to receive suggestions with an open mind, to put good ideas into prompt effect, and to pass them on to others.

New approaches will bring new problems, but I know we have the management ability to solve them. Our Company and our country will face far greater problems if we and other employers fail to do what we can to help disadvantaged people overcome the barriers that keep them from sharing in the abundance of the American economy.

The achievement of genuinely equal opportunity is the most urgent task our nation faces. Ford Motor Company is pledged to provide equal opportunity in its own operations, but that commitment can be only as good as the personal performance of each of us. I therefore ask you to accept a full share of the responsibility for making Ford Motor Company an equal opportunity business in every sense of the term.

Henry Ford II
Chairman of the Board

182

Notes to Chapters

Chapter 1

[1] From a speech April 30, 1968, in Flint, Michigan, before the American Institute of Industrial Engineers.

[2] Editors of *Fortune, The Negro and the City.* New York: Time-Life Books, 1968.

[3] *Report of the National Advisory Commission on Civil Disorders.* New York: Bantam Books, Inc., 1968.

[4] "Business and the Urban Crisis," *Fortune,* January 1968.

[5] "Setting a New Course in Meeting Race Violence," *U.S. News and World Report,* July 8, 1968, p. 39.

[6] *Report of the National Advisory Commission on Civil Disorders, op. cit.*

[7] *Ibid.*

Chapter 2

[1] Herbert Northrup and Richard L. Rowan, *The Negro and Employment Opportunity.* Ann Arbor: Bureau of Industrial Relations, University of Michigan, 1965, p. 1.

[2] Quoted in "Business and the Urban Crisis," a McGraw-Hill Special Report, *Business Week,* February 3, 1968, p. C4.

Chapter 3

[1] "Speaking Out," *The Saturday Evening Post,* April 20, 1968.

[2] *Ibid.*

Chapter 4

[1] Harold H. Martin, "The Fires of Summer," *The Saturday Evening Post,* April 20, 1968.
[2] *Ibid.*
[3] Cited in Peter Paret and John W. Shy, *Guerillas in the Sixties.* New York: Praeger Paperbacks, 1962.
[4] *Ibid.*
[5] *Ibid.*

Chapter 5

[1] Garth Mangum, ed., *The Manpower Revolution.* New York: Doubleday & Co., Inc., 1965.
[2] *Ibid.*
[3] Sol Stern, "When the Black GI Comes Back from Vietnam," *The New York Times Magazine,* March 28, 1968.
[4] *Ibid.*
[5] "The Black Panthers," *Ramparts,* June 29, 1968.
[6] The Associated Press, June 27, 1968.

Chapter 6

[1] Sar Levitan, "Lessons We Could Have Learned from the Anti-Poverty Efforts," *Poverty and Human Resources Abstracts,* Ann Arbor: Institute of Labor and Industrial Relations, University of Michigan—Wayne State University, January–February 1968.
[2] Frances Piven, "The Demonstration Project—A Federal Strategy for Local Change," in G. A. Brager and F. P. Purcell, eds., *Community Action Against Poverty.* New Haven: College and University Press, 1967.
[3] M. Rein and S. M. Miller, "The Demonstration Project as a Strategy of Change," in M. Zald, ed., *Organizing for Community Change.* Chicago: Quadrangle Books, 1967.

Chapter 7

[1] "New Acting CORE Head Asks Black Ghetto Rule," *Michigan Daily* (Ann Arbor), June 29, 1968, p. 1.
[2] *Ibid.*
[3] *Report of the National Advisory Commission on Civil Disorders, op. cit.*

184

[4] Stokely Carmichael and Charles V. Hamilton, *Black Power.* New York: Vintage Books, 1968.

Chapter 8

[1] Joseph Schumpeter, *Capitalism, Socialism and Democracy.* New York, Harper & Bros., 1942.

[2] "The U.S. Negro Market in 1967," *Sponsor,* July 1967.

[3] Sophia McDowell, "How Anti-White Are Negro Youth?" *Education,* March 1968.

[4] *Ibid.*

Chapter 9

[1] Henry Ford II, "The National Alliance of Businessmen," *Michigan Business Review,* July 1968.

[2] United Press International, July 3, 1968.

[3] Ray Marshall, "Job Problems of Negroes," in *The Negro and Employment Opportunity, op. cit.*

Chapter 11

[1] E. Ruda and L. E. Albright, "Racial Differences on Selection Instruments Related to Subsequent Job Performance," *Personnel Psychology,* XXI, 1 (Spring 1968).

Chapter 12

[1] Theodore H. Kheel, "Increasing Employment Opportunity in the Printing and Electrical Trades," in Northrup and Rowan, *op. cit.*

[2] *Op. cit.,* p. 12.

[3] A. H. Raskin, "The Working Man Is a Snob," *The Saturday Evening Post,* May 18, 1968.

[4] Julius Dobson, "Speaking Out: Uncle Sam is a Bigot," *The Saturday Evening Post,* April 20, 1968.

[5] J. P. Wernette, *Growth and Prosperity Without Inflation.* New York: Ronald Press, 1961.

[6] Arthur Burns, *Prosperity Without Inflation.* Buffalo, N.Y.: Economics Books, 1958.

Suggested Readings

Report of the National Advisory Commission on Civil Disorders, Bantam Books, Inc., New York, 1968.

This report, also called the Kerner Commission Report, is by the Commission on Civil Disorders appointed by President Johnson in July 1967. It is a basic source document for any person studying the urban crisis with on-the-spot investigations and population studies. This is not only the primer on urban riots and black uprisings, but also an advanced text and reference volume.

The Negro in America, The Condensed Version of Gunnar Myrdal's *An American Dilemma,* by Arnold Rose, with Foreword by Gunnar Myrdal. Harper Torchbooks, Harper & Row, Publishers, New York, 1964.

This book was originally published in 1948 from *An American Dilemma,* and is a classic study by a Swedish sociologist on the problem of blacks in America. It explains in depth the history of the black experience in America and discusses major problems of the blacks. The underlying social effects of segregation are spelled out in a way which makes the riots of the sixties intelligible and even predictable.

The Negro and Employment Opportunity, Herbert Northrup and Richard L. Rowan, Bureau of Industrial Relations, University of Michigan, Ann Arbor, Michigan, 1965.

The conclusion of this germinal study by two professors from the University of Pennsylvania is the need of employment for black people. The book includes articles by Roy Wilkins and Marelon Puryear, prominent black leaders; and by experts on labor relations and the jobs and labor market problems of blacks. Political approaches are surveyed, followed by several companies' experiences in employing and training blacks at such firms as General Motors, General Electric, Honeywell, Western Electric, and southern textile firms. Other topics included are union policies, community approaches, drop-outs, and the status of blacks in business and professional leadership positions. The book tells how some business leaders have assumed leadership in the provision of jobs for all blacks. This is a basic reading book for company persons interested in the many problems of hiring blacks.

Black Power, The Politics of Liberation in America, Stokely Carmichael and Charles V. Hamilton, Vintage Books, a division of Random House, Inc., New York, 1968.

This book, written by Carmichael, a leading black militant organizer, and Hamilton, a political scientist from Roosevelt University in Chicago, describes the advantages of black people organizing themselves to assume power over their own destinies. Black Power, the authors state, is a "political framework and ideology which represents the last reasonable opportunity for this society to work out its problems short of prolonged guerrilla warfare." This book is essential reading for viewing the full dimension of the black militant's rage, and the possibilities of violence to counter what black leaders see as white oppression.

To Be Equal, Whitney Young, McGraw Hill Book Co., New York, 1964.

This is a moderate statement by the head of the Urban League which has a policy of living within the existing framework and adopting moderation to move the existing institutions toward integration. Whitney Young is a black man and is accepted by corporation chiefs and major establishment leaders. He insists on the need for change, yet accepts the existing system.

187

Index

Activist movement, 69-71
Adams, Charles, 116
Aerojet General, 116
Africa, migration of blacks to, 91
Alternatives to violence, 14-17
    government programs, 15, 32-42
    hiring blacks, 16-17, 168-169
    military service, 17, 62-77
    new programs, 16, 78-88
    riot control, 15-16, 48-61
    riots, 3-18, 48-61
American Insurance Association,
    8, 10
Area Redevelopment program, 36
Atlanta, Georgia, disorders, 6
Automation, effects of, 37

Baltimore riots, 7, 8
Banes, Arthur, 116
Barfield, Johnny, 97
Birmingham, Alabama, disorders,
    4, 128
Black business, 91, 94, 97-98
    aid to managers, 97-98
    new business creation, 97-98
"Black is beautiful," 24
Black militants, 73-76
    returning veterans, 68-72
    revolutionary aims, 74
Black Panthers, 74
    revolutionary aims, 74, 76
Black Power, 89-98
    aims, 90
    appeals to violence, 90
    corporations and, 93-98
    definition, 89
    economic effects, 91
    effect on blacks, 90
    militarism, 92-93

Newark conference (1967), 92-93
    political power, 90-91
    separatism, 91-92
Blackstone Rangers, 57, 74, 75-76,
    86
    OEO grant to, 75-76
Blount, Winton M., 9
Bogalusa, La., 5
Boston, Mass., black population,
    20
Boycotts, by blacks, 104-105
Boyd, Virgil, 115, 118
Brown, Rap, 74
Buckley, William, 166
Burns, Arthur, 175-176
Buying behavior of blacks, 103-104
Buying power of blacks, 99-100

Cambridge, Md., disorders, 4
Capitalism, 101-102
Carmichael, Stokely, 70, 74, 95
Castro, Fidel, 59, 60
Cato, Charles, 69
Chemical MACE, 51
Chicago (Illinois), Blackstone
    Rangers, 74, 75
    crime among blacks, 30
    riots, 4, 5, 7, 8, 55
Chrysler Corporation, 114, 115,
    119, 174
Cincinnati, Ohio, 6, 11
Cities, migration of blacks to, 20-21
    poverty of blacks, 26-28
    urbanization of blacks, 20-21
    See also Urban crisis
Civil rights movement, 50, 55
Civil Service Commission, 43-44
Clausewitz, Carl Von, 58
Clay, Cassius, 92

189

Cleveland, Ohio, 4, 21
 riots, 4, 5, 11, 56
Cole, Edward, 174
Community Action Program, 86
 strategy for local change, 86-88
Concentrated Employment
 Program (CEP), 117
Congress of Racial Equality
 (CORE), 89
Consumption, 109-111
 accelerator system, 109, 111
 investments and, 109
 multiplier effect, 109
Cooperation between government
 and industry, 117-121
Corporations, executive actions,
 113-129
 hiring hard-core blacks, 63,
 113-129
 interest in Black Power, 93-98
 job-training for veterans, 68
 policy decisions, 113-129
 providing leadership, 94
 responsibilities of, 61, 63, 94,
 113-129
 use of government aid, 125-127
 See also Management;
 Private Sector
Credit availability, 107
Crime rate, 29-31

Daley, Richard (Mayor of Chicago),
 50-51
Day, William, 55
de Gaulle, General Charles,
 55-56
Demonstration projects, 16, 39-40,
 46, 78-88
 cost-effectiveness, 85-87
 government funding, 79, 80-85
 limitations, 84-85
 local agitation aspects, 86

research funds for, 80-82
 types of, 82-83
Depressions, hedges against, 158-
 176
 resources for averting, 174-176
 See also Recessions
Detroit, Michigan, 21, 112
 effect of hiring blacks, 112
 New Detroit Committee, 55, 114
 riots, 4, 5, 6-7
Detroit Edison, 112
Dobson, Julius, 171
Drop-outs, 126
 government programs for, 37
 hiring, 114

Education for hard-core
 unemployed, 37-40
 retraining courses, 38-39, 46
Elizabeth, N.J., disorders, 6
Employment patterns, 122-124
 aggressive recruitment, 123-124
 federal programs, 34-37
 preferential practices, 124,
 168-169
Equal employment opportunity,
 43-44
Equal Employment Opportunity
 Commission, 172-173
Ex-convicts, hiring, 114, 117, 126
Executive Order of September 24,
 1965, 42, 44
Exploitation of blacks, 94-96

Family life in ghetto areas, 28-31
Federal Communications
 Commission, 170-171
Federal Reserve System, 175
Federal troops, riot training, 50
Fisk University, 5
Ford, Henry, II, 82, 131-133, 158
 "Blue Letter," 115

on hiring blacks, 26, 115
Ford Motor Company, 128, 152
  economic effects of hiring
    blacks, 82, 109-112
  induction program, 145-147
  training programs, 119, 174
Foremen, responsibilities of, 142-156
  absentee problem, 149-150
  following through on, 150-151
  induction program, 145-147
  job-instruction training, 145, 147-148
  meetings for, 142-150
  special actions and programs, 148-149
  telephone calling programs, 149
Full employment, economic
  effects, 108-112

Garvey, Marcus, 91-92
General Motors, 3-4, 112, 114
  training programs, 173-174
Genocide, 56-57
German concentration camps, 56
Ghetto areas, 96-97
  crime, 30
  declining quality of life, 28-31
  health conditions, 30-31
  role of corporations, 88, 96-97
  slum merchants, 94-95
Goldberg, Arthur N., 36-37
Government agencies, discriminatory hiring practices, 42-45, 170-173
  paucity of training, 173-174
Government aid, in hiring
  disadvantaged, 125-127
  limitations, 125-127
  for private programs, 117-118
Government programs, 32-42
  Area Redevelopment, 36

barriers to, 46-47
cost-effectiveness of, 33-36, 45-47
discrimination in employment, 42-45, 170-173
diversity of approach, 33-35
enforcement mechanism, 46
employment programs, 33-35
hiring black employees, 42-45
Manpower Development and
  Training Act, 36-40
patterns of employment, 42-45
poverty programs, 34-35
strategy for local change, 86-88
Study of Minority Group
  Employment, 43-45
United States Employment
  Service, 41-42
Griffith, William, 75
Guerrilla warfare, 57-61
  city as base of operations, 60
  Communist efforts, 59
  conditions for, 58
  infiltration of military and police, 60
  objectives of, 59-60
  returning veterans and, 69-73
  support of population, 73
Guevara, Che, 60
Gun control legislation, 52-53

Harris, Louis, 167
Harvey, James, 3
Hatcher, Carl, 91
Hiring hard-core unemployed, 16-17
  biased or exclusive policies, 25-26
  demonstration programs, 154-155
  developing plans for, 133-137

Hiring hard-core unemployed
  (Continued)
  effect of recession on, 157-176
  by government agencies, 42-45,
    170-173
  government aid, 125-127
  inability to read signs, 153
  instilling dependability, 152-153
  job performance, 153
  on-the-job supervision, 152-155
  middle management programs,
    130-141
  opportunities for business, 17
  policies of top management,
    113-129
  preferential treatment, 124,
    168-169
  resentment of whites, 141, 153
  responsibilities of foreman,
    142-156
  responsibilities of private
    sector, 47, 61
  returning veterans, 68-72
  riots, effect of, 114-115
  selection standards, 115, 124,
    155-156, 168-169
  statement of policies, 121-124
  supervision problems, 152-155
  tax consequences, 46-47
  training, 16
    See also Training programs
  turnover records, 154
  underemployment problem,
    24-26
  union relations and, 154,
    164-170
  upgrading skills levels, 159-164
Hobson, Julius, 43-44
Hoess, Rudolf, 56
Horowitz, Julius, 31
Houston, Texas, 6, 21
Hudson, J. L., Jr., 114

Hudson Department Store, Detroit,
  100, 108, 114

Illiteracy, 153
Incomes of blacks, 27-28
Innis, Roy, 89-90
Insurance companies, investments
  in ghetto housing, 94
Integration or segregation, 94

Jackson State College,
  Mississippi, 5
Jacksonville, Florida, 4
Jersey City, New Jersey, 6
Job Corps, 35, 40, 126-127
JOBS (Job Opportunity in the
  Business Sector), 118-121
Johnson, Lyndon B., 42, 52-53, 117

Kansas City, 8
Kennedy, John F., 53
Kennedy, Robert F., 53
Kerner Commission, 11-12, 53, 80,
  145
Kheel, Theodore, 162-163
Killingsworth, Charles, 37
King, Martin Luther, Jr., 3, 7, 15, 50

Labor unions, 164-170
  apprenticeship training for
    blacks, 123, 162-164
  conservative workers, 165-170
  discrimination in craft unions,
    162-163
  liberal employers and, 167-170
  resentment of white workers,
    141, 166
  USES and, 41
Law and order, 29-31
  Safe Streets Act, 52-54
Lawrence, T. E., 59
Leadership, black, 29, 58, 70-71

corporations and, 94
Lemberg Center for the Study of
    Violence, 10
Levitan, Sar, 84
Lindsay, John V., 85, 166
Lockheed Aircraft, 116-117
Look Magazine, 40
Looting and firebombing, 7, 50-51
Lopez, Felix, 155
Los Angeles, riot in Watts, 5

Machaver, Bill, 124
McKenzie, Gavin, 167
McNamara, Robert S., 17, 66-67
Malcolm X, 92
Management, alternative policies,
    14-18
  executive actions, 113-129
  personal commitment, 115
  policy decisions, 124-129
  responsibilities, 13-14
      See also Corporations
Mangum, Garth, 84, 85
Manpower Development and
    Training Act (MDTA), 36-40
  cost of, 85
  in-plant courses, 117
  qualification rationale, 42, 44
Mao Tse-tung, 58-59
Market power of blacks, 91, 99-112
  buying behavior, 103-104
  buying power, 99-101, 104-108
  consumer information, 105-106
  consumption patterns, 106-107
  corporate policies and, 104-108
  discriminatory pricing, 108
  economic potential, 101-102,
    108-112
  effect of price, 107-108
  size of black market, 99-101
  use of boycott, 104-105
Marshall, Ray, 24-25, 122-123, 165

Martin, Harold, 54
Memphis, Tenn., 9, 21
Meredith, James, 90
Miami, Florida, 51
Middle-class bias, 40, 44
Middle-class blacks, 27
Middle management programs,
    130-141
  control and reporting systems,
    139-141
  organization for action, 133-137
  plans and programs, 137-139
  statement of objectives, 131-133
Military service for blacks, 17,
    62-77
  casualty rate, 67, 70
  enlisted occupation, 64-65
  limitations, 17, 72-73
  Project 100,000, 67-68
  Project Transition, 68
  qualification tests, 66
  reenlistment rate, 67
  remedial programs for
    previously unfit, 66-68
  returning veterans, 68-72
  solution for unemployment, 62,
    72-73
  Vietnam War, 65-67, 70
Miller, S. M., 87
Mills, Wilbur, 15
Mississippi, riots in, 4, 5
Moynihan, Daniel, 41, 67, 84, 167
Muhammed Ali, 92
Muslims, 92

National Alliance of Businessmen,
    33, 82, 117-121
  government cooperation and,
    117-118
  100,000 placed in jobs, 33, 82,
    117
National Guard, 8-9, 15-16, 48

National Guard *(Continued)*
 riot control training, 49-50
National Negro Marketing
 Institute, 104
Nationalism, black, 90-92
Negative income tax, 119-121
Neighborhood Youth Corps, 35, 40
New Orleans, La., 21
New York City, 30, 166
 riots, 4, 8, 11
New York Times, The, 25, 69, 166
Newark, N.J., 6, 21, 92-93
Newspapers, 9, 106
Newton, Huey, 74
Nixon, Richard, 47

OEO (Office of Economic
 Opportunity), 33, 83
 Community Action Programs, 86
 cost of, 45
 Job Corps camps, 126
Organization for action, 133-137
 staff meetings, 135-137
 written communications, 133-
 134
Organization of Afro-American
 Unity, 92

Paris riots, 55-56
Patterson, N.J., 9-10
Philadelphia, Pa., 4, 21
Phillippe, Gerard, 114-115
Pittsburgh, Pa., 7, 8, 9
Piven, Frances, 86-87
Police and riot control, 8-9, 11, 12,
 15-16, 52
Policy statements, 121-124,
 128-129
Political power of blacks, 90-91, 94
Poor People's March, 60
Population growth of blacks, 21-23,
 99-100

Poverty and Human Resources
 Abstracts (PHRA), 81-82
Poverty of blacks, 26-28
 causes, 19-20
Poverty programs, 15, 32-42, 80-82,
 86
 cost of, 15, 45-47
 list of, 34-35
Pride in race, 24, 31, 60
Private sector, 93-97
 black veterans hired by, 72-73
 effect on purchasing power, 88
 inner city renewal, 96
 responsibility for hiring blacks,
 47, 61
Programs for hiring hard-core,
 117-156
 middle management, 130-141
 policy decisions, 117-129
 responsibilities of foreman,
 142-156
Purchasing power of blacks,
 99-100

Racism, 57, 70, 89
Randolph, A. Philip, 45
Raskin, A. H., 166
Recessions, 157-176
 effects on blacks, 157-176
 hedges against, 158-159
 resources to snub, 174-176
 unskilled laid off first, 161-163
 upgrading skills levels,
 159-164
Resurrection City, 9, 60
Riot control, 8-10, 12-13, 48-61
 counterstrategies, 51
 dangers in, 15-16, 54-57
 nonviolent protest, 59, 60
 tactics and weapons, 49-52,
 54-55
 training in, 49-52

Riots, 3-18, 50-51
  alternatives to, 14-18
  basic pattern, 11-13
  characteristics of rioters, 12-13,
    31
  deaths and injuries, 6-8, 10
  property damage, 6-8, 10-11
Roche, James, 114
Ross, Arthur, 157
Russell, Carlos, 70

Safe Streets and Crime Control
    Act, 52-54
Schumpeter, Joseph, 101
Selection standards, 114, 155-156
Selma, Alabama, 5
Seniority system, 161-162
Separatism, black, 91-92, 94
Skinner, Norman, 103-104
Social disintegration, 28-31, 54
Social problems, corporate
    commitment, 113-129
Spina, Dominick, 48, 51
Stern, Sol, 69, 71-72
Stokes, Carl, 90
Student uprisings, 5-6, 19
Summer positions, 117

Tax consequences of poverty
    programs, 15, 46, 85-86
Tax surcharge of 1968, 157, 175
Teen-agers, employment of, 23-25,
    117
Telephone calling programs, 149
Testing programs, discriminatory,
    42, 44-45, 114, 159, 171-172
Townsend, Lynn, 114
Training programs, 16, 38-40,
    115-121
  government agencies, 173-174
  government grants for, 117-121,
    155

MDTA programs, 36-40
  pre-employment, 114-117, 155
  tuition refund payments, 174
  upgrading skills levels, 159-164
Turnover rate of blacks, 150, 154,
    156

Underemployment, 24-26, 39
  upgrading skills, 44, 88, 159-164
Unemployment among blacks,
    23-26, 153-164
  economic effects of full
    employment, 108-112
  federal programs, 33
    See also Government
    programs
  military service as solution,
    62-67
  rate for, 23
United Automobile Workers, 110,
    164
United States, Health, Education,
    and Welfare Department
    (HEW), 33-35, 37, 43, 83
  Housing and Urban
    Development (HUD), 33
  Labor Department, 41-42, 84,
    118
United States Chamber of
    Commerce, 9, 81-82
United States Employment Service
    (USES), 41-42
Upgrading skills, 97-98, 159-164
Upjohn Institute for Unemployment
    Research, 82
Urban Coalition, 132
Urban crisis, 19-31, 132
  alternative solutions, 14-17
  causes, 19-20
  corporate policies, 113-129
  declining quality of life, 28-31
  federal programs, 32-42

Urban crisis *(Continued)*
  inner city renewal, 97
  migration to cities, 20-21
  population growth, 21-23
Urban League, 71
Urbanization of blacks, 19, 20-21

Vietnam War, 65-67, 70
  black casualties, 65-66, 67, 70

Wallace, George, 57, 166
Washington, Larry, 152-155, 164
Washington, Walter, 9
Washington, D.C., 3, 7, 8-9, 21, 43
Watts Manufacturing Company,
  116, 126
Watts riot, 5

Wernette, Philip, 174-176
Westmoreland, General William,
  68
Wheeler, Dr. Al, 51
Whites, fear of job competition, 25
  flight to suburbs, 19, 21
  racism, 57, 70, 89
  resistance of, 141, 165-170
Wilkins, Roy, 91
Wiretapping, 52-53
Wirtz, Willard, 41
Working mothers, 29

Young, Whitney, Jr., 71

Zisch, William, 116